THE DELIBERATE DEATH
OF A POLISH PRIEST

For Halina Szpiro

RONALD HARWOOD

THE DELIBERATE DEATH
OF A POLISH PRIEST

A play based on the transcripts of a trial
and other material arising out of the murder of
Father Jerzy Popieluszko

AMBER LANE PRESS ● OXFORD
APPLAUSE THEATRE BOOK PUBLISHERS ● NEW YORK

All rights whatsoever in this play are strictly reserved
and application for performance etc. should be made before
rehearsal to:

Judy Daish Associates Ltd.
83 Eastbourne Mews
London W2 6LQ

No performance may be given unless a licence has been obtained.

First published in 1985 by
Amber Lane Press Ltd.
9 Middle Way
Oxford OX2 7LH

Published in the USA by
Applause Theatre Book Publishers
211 West 71 Street
New York, N.Y. 10023

ISBN: 0 906399 63 7 in the UK

ISBN: 0-87910-262-4 in the USA

Library of Congress Cataloging-in-Publication Data

Harwood, Ronald, 1934-
   The deliberate death of a Polish priest.

   1. Popiełuszko, Jerzy, 1947-1984--Drama. 2. Poland--
History--1980-   --Drama. I. Title.
PR6058.A73D4 1985   822'.914   85-26653
ISBN 0-87910-262-4 (pbk.)

Printed in Great Britain by
Cotswold Press Ltd., Oxford

Copyright © Paracier Holdings Ltd., 1985

CHARACTERS

FATHER JERZY POPIELUSZKO
THE JUDGE
THE PROSECUTOR
JAN OLSZEWSKI, an Auxiliary Prosecutor
GRZEGORZ PIOTROWSKI, former Captain in the Interior
Ministry
LESZEK PEKALA, former Lieutenant in the Interior Ministry
WALDEMAR CHMIELEWSKI, former Lieutenant in the
Interior Ministry
ADAM PIETRUSZKA, former Colonel in the Interior Ministry
BARBARA MARCZUK, a Defence Counsel
WALDEMAR CHROSTOWSKI, Fr. Popieluszko's driver
BARBARA STORY, a secretary in the Interior Ministry
GENERAL ZENON PLATEK, Head of Department in the
Interior Ministry
PROFESSOR MARIA BYRDY, a pathologist
A GUARD
A COURT OFFICIAL

The play is set in the Provincial Court of Torun. The dock should
be the main focus of the action. (In the course of the trial a screen
is required for the viewing of film.)

All the words of Father Popieluszko, the accused and the witnesses are their own.

In the case of the lawyers and the Judge, I have occasionally
added questions in order to clarify otherwise long and complex
statements. Their opinions, tactics and points of view, however,
are expressed in their own words.

Ronald Harwood, 1985

The Deliberate Death of a Polish Priest was first presented at the Almeida Theatre, London, on 17 October 1985 by Primetime Television in association with the Almeida Theatre, with the following cast:

FATHER JERZY POPIELUSZKO	Struan Rodger
THE JUDGE	Garfield Morgan
THE PROSECUTOR	John Shrapnel
JAN OLSZEWSKI	Alfred Lynch
GRZEGORZ PIOTROWSKI	Stuart Wilson
LESZEK PEKALA	Jim Broadbent
WALDEMAR CHMIELEWSKI	Roger Lloyd Pack
ADAM PIETRUSZKA	Derek Newark
BARBARA MARCZUK	Janis Winters
WALDEMAR CHROSTOWSKI	Brian Cox
BARBARA STORY	Tessa Wojtczak
GENERAL ZENON PLATEK	Michael Graham Cox
PROFESSOR MARIA BYRDY	Rosamund Greenwood
A GUARD	Tim Stone
COURT OFFICIAL	Kit Jackson

Designed by Eileen Diss
Directed by Kevin Billington

ACT ONE

Dim light on the Court, so that all those seated there are shadowy, faceless.

Downstage, with his back to the audience, sits WALDEMAR CHROSTOWSKI, *not part of the Court but, for the moment, an observer. He is watching the witness box.*

Light grows on the witness box.

The priest, FATHER JERZY POPIELUSZKO, *robed for Mass, enters and goes into the witness box.*

He is thirty-seven years old, slight of build, and with a somewhat diffident, gentle demeanour. He is no great orator but speaks with intensity and burning conviction.

POPIELUSZKO: So that you may know the *provocateurs* among you, our stewards today will be wearing green armbands. I don't have to remind you that this is a Mass for the Homeland and not a political rally. I ask all the faithful not to listen to the *provocateurs* who are here among us and who call for a demonstration after the Mass. Let us agree that after the Mass only the *provocateurs* will sing and shout slogans outside the church. Let us force them to go away empty-handed. And to the *provocateurs* I say, brothers, you were ordered to come here, but I ask you to serve truth and justice, keep your self-respect and let the faithful depart in peace.

[*He smooths out his notes. He crosses himself.*]

I would like us today to turn our thoughts towards truth and justice. The just man is he who is guided by love and truth. Where there is absence of love and truth, hatred and oppression take their place and where there is hatred and oppression there can be no question of justice. That is why injustice is so painfully apparent in countries where authority is held not in a spirit of love and service, but through slavery and oppression, by monstrous censorship which bans all truthful and courageous words or ideas. It censors what was written by pens soaked in truth. And, after all, words, in order to be alive, have to be truthful. Too many wrongs — both social and personal — have been suffered from the fact that in this country justice is wielded without love and truth and often turns into blatant injustice. Justice must denounce the restrictions on the freedom of the individual. Justice demands that working people should have the freedom to join trades unions which can best help them. Justice grants us the right and the duty to demand freedom for all those who have been arrested for their convictions. We further demand the unconditional release of all those who have now been imprisoned for thirty–one months without trial or sentence. But we must never forget that that which is in the heart, which is deep within man, cannot be destroyed by decrees or bans. I think we could call to mind here the story told of one of the poor African states, where the country's leader forbade its citizens to use the word 'hunger' under threat of severe penalties and then announced to the world that in his country the problem of hunger had been solved. Similarly, in our country, the word 'Solidarity' should not be treated with contempt. It is a word of which the whole world speaks with reverence, for Solidarity hopes to satisfy the hunger of the human heart, the hunger for love, justice and truth. In order to remain spiritually free men, we must live in truth. The source of our captivity lies in the fact that we allow lies to reign, that we do not denounce them, that we do not protest against their existence every day of our lives. So let us now consider our own hearts, and ask ourselves how far we have the courage to demand justice, and how far each of us helps to create true justice, beginning with ourselves, our families, our social environment. For often, it is our own moral indifference which inspires injustice.

[*Light begins to grow on those in the Court.*]

And never, never must we fight by means of violence. Violence is a sign of weakness. Whatever cannot win by influencing the heart tries to win by means of violence. The most splendid and lasting battles known to history are the battles of human thought. An idea that needs weapons to survive will die by itself. We must overcome fear. Fear stems from threats. We fear suffering. We fear losing material good. We fear losing freedom or our work. And then we act contrary to our conscience, thus muzzling truth. We can overcome fear only if we accept suffering in the name of a greater value. Christ told his followers: 'Be not afraid of them that kill the body, and after that have no more that they can do'.

[*He bows his head and prays. While he does so, light grows slowly on the Court. The* PROSECUTOR, PIETRASZYNSKI, *rises.*]

PROSECUTOR: The Provincial Prosecutor's Office in Torun charges: Grzegorz Piotrowski—

[PIOTROWSKI *stands in the dock. He is thirty-three, arrogant, detached.*]

Leszek Pekala—

[PEKALA *stands. He is thirty-two, strongly built, tense.*]

Waldemar Marek Chmielewski—

[CHMIELEWSKI *stands. He, too, is well-built, aged twenty-nine. He is in the throes of a nervous breakdown. He shivers and trembles, and a pulse explodes uncontrollably in his cheek.*]

—that in the early hours of 20th October 1984 at Gorsk in the Province of Torun, acting jointly and in collusion, with intent to take his life, they deceitfully stopped on the highway Jerzy Popieluszko travelling in a Volkswagen Golf motor-car, rendered him unconscious with blows from fists and a wooden club, gagged him, tied his hands and legs with a rope, placed him in the boot of a Fiat 125P motor-car and took him to Torun and along the highway, in connection with Jerzy Popieluszko's attempts to free himself, they again beat him, gagged him, tied his hands and legs with rope and finally placed a loop of rope around his neck and tied a sack containing stones to his legs, and having taken him to a dam in the vicinity of Wloclawek, threw him into the water, causing his death through suffocation.

[POPIELUSZKO *crosses himself and then descends from the witness box. The light on him fades.*]

[CHROSTOWSKI *turns to the audience as* POPIELUSZKO *exits.*]

CHROSTOWSKI: There are three main charges against them. The first, as the Prosecutor's just said, is that they killed the priest. The second, that they tried to kill me. My name is Waldemar Chrostowski. In my spare time I was the priest's driver. He was my confessor. But, you could say, we were also friends. The third charge relates to something they did a week earlier. Again, I was involved. I'm driving Father Popieluszko and a colleague. It's night and the priest's asleep in the back. We've just left Gdansk and we're heading for Warsaw. Piotrowski steps out into the road. He has a stone in his hand. He's taking aim. He wants to smash my windscreen. But I drive hard at him and he misses. That's on the 13th October. A week later, on the night of the 19th-20th, they try again. Now, they plead not guilty. They say they had no intention of killing innocent people but only wanted to deprive them of their freedom. Anyway, the fact is, that the second time, on 19th October, Father Popieluszko died, you might say, while in their company. And, of course, there's another man in the dock.

PROSECUTOR: The Provincial Prosecutor's Office in Torun charges that Adam Pietruszka—

> [COLONEL PIETRUSZKA *rises. He is the son of peasants, tough, in his late forties.*]

—in September and October 1984 in Warsaw, using his position as deputy director of a department at the Ministry of Internal Affairs, induced his subordinates to kidnap in a particularly cruel manner and to murder Jerzy Popieluszko, and further that after the act was committed by them he entered upon activities impeding the discovery of the perpetrators, contrary to Article 18 Clause—

> [*A sudden blackout.*]
> [*Confusion in the Court.*]
> [*Light on* CHROSTOWSKI.]

CHROSTOWSKI: A power failure. [*He smiles.*] The lights, like the men in the dock, aren't always efficient. In the dark, then, the Court waits for the proceedings to continue. Outside, against the wall of a nearby church, people have put together an altar dedicated to the priest. Hundreds of them, men, women and children, lay flowers and pray there, until the police cordon around the Court is widened so that it cuts off that side of the church. But it doesn't take long for the people to hammer together another altar on the church wall beyond the cordon. Father Jerzy was more than a priest. All over the world people cry out against his murder. People who never saw him or heard him. But they knew him. He touched their lives. He gave them — well — he was more than a priest. And that's why he died.

[*Candles and torches glow here and there, dimly lighting the Court.*]

Security is tough, so, on the day of the power failure, all the searches and frisking is done by candle and torchlight.

[*A torch held by the* COURT OFFICIAL *illuminates the* GUARD *frisking* OLSZEWSKI.]

The man being searched is Jan Olszewski. He is called an Auxiliary Prosecutor but, in fact, he represents the priest's family. That's the Prosecutor, and that's the Judge. The woman is Counsel for the Defence. There are five journalists from the West present. Polish radio and television record the proceedings and each night they broadcast edited excerpts. Yes, edited. [*He smiles wryly.*] And everyone is asking why? Why are they having this trial for the whole world to witness? And no-one knows the answer for certain. Perhaps they had no choice. Perhaps there was nothing else they could do. And there's an old story going around. See if I can get it right. It happened before the war. A Frenchman, Pierre Laval, something like that, he's visiting Stalin. Laval says, 'Can't you do something to encourage religion and the Catholics in Russia? It would help me so much with the Pope'. 'Oho!' Stalin says. 'The Pope! How many divisions has *he* got?' They should have come to Poland.

[*Lights snap on.*]
[*Relief in the Court.*]
[*While the Court settles:*]

So where does it all begin? With Adam Pietruszka, perhaps? Deputy Head of *a* Department in the Interior Ministry, and although it's not said officially which department, everybody knows it's a special group that deals with Church affairs. Pietruszka, former Colonel in the Security Service and, like all the accused, the Captain and the two lieutenants, now reduced to the rank of private and expelled from the Polish Communist Party. The name Pietruszka, by the way, means parsley. [*He squeezes a smile.*] Does the priest's death begin with him?

[COLONEL PIETRUSZKA *stands in the dock.* CHROSTOWSKI *sits and watches.*]

PROSECUTOR: Does the accused understand the charge levelled against him in the act of indictment?

COLONEL: I do.

PROSECUTOR: Does the accused admit to committing the act of which he is accused?

COLONEL: No, I do not, may it please the Court, admit to committing that action because the accusation in its entirety is based on the slanders of this man, Grzegorz Piotrowski.

PROSECUTOR: The accused does not admit the charge. Does the accused want to testify? I'm asking, because I don't want there to be any doubts later on.

COLONEL: Yes, I do want to testify.

JUDGE: I notify all who testify of the penal responsibility borne by persons who give false testimony.

COLONEL: If the Court permits, I would like at the outset to show the scale, the importance of the phenomena, the importance of the matter conventionally linked with Father Popieluszko. There are a dozen or so priests in this country of Father Popieluszko's type: that is to say, priests who wear a cross on their breast and an unambiguous hatred in their hearts; priests who exploit their function as clergy to present that hatred; priests who want to involve the faithful in this. So, on or about 20th September last year, I asked Capt — [*He cuts himself short.*] — I asked Piotrowski to come to my office. There was also a section head from the Office of Internal Affairs present. His name's Wolski. The reason for this meeting — let us call it a conference — was the question of publicly hostile speeches or sermons by priests or, to be more precise, the effectiveness of our counteractions to the politically harmful sermons by priests.

PROSECUTOR: Why was there a need for such a meeting?

COLONEL: There had been an increase in this type of sermon, in organizing so-called Masses for the Homeland. Those Masses had a misleading title. They turned out, in essence, to be quasi-political rallies, to say nothing of the content of what was proclaimed from the pulpit. And, as a rule, a certain type of aggressive behaviour accompanied these Masses. I'm not talking about the behaviour of the faithful because I wouldn't like to hurt people who really are believers. But I'm referring to the aggressive behaviour *after* the Masses, people leaving the church, since I understand and assume, maybe a bit prematurely, maybe a bit *a priori*, that a person who really does believe would not take part in those excesses afterwards, demonstrations, shouting slogans and so on.

PROSECUTOR: Tell us what was said at that meeting between you, section head Wolski and the accused, Piotrowski.

COLONEL: Well, I commenced my reflections regarding the speeches being made by another priest, Father Malkowski, speeches that contained elements of hatred towards people who think differently, elements of hatred towards people unconnected with the Church, and, above all, elements of hatred towards people associated with a world outlook and I'd say not only Marxist. We consulted, Your Honour, the opinions of priest-professors from Church scientific circles, from the Papal Academy in Cracow, people who represented all the theological disciplines.

PROSECUTOR: And what were the opinions of the learned priest-professors concerning these sermons?

COLONEL: All of them unanimously stated that, in the theological dimension, these sermons clearly breached doctrinal principles, particularly the slogan: 'Love thine enemies'.

PROSECUTOR: And you presented those arguments at the meeting?

COLONEL: Yes. I stated that there was now a need to assess those sermons in legal terms.

PROSECUTOR: And what was Piotrowski's opinion?

COLONEL: At that time, he, of course, agreed with me, but said that he thought the stress should, however, be put more on Father Popieluszko.

PROSECUTOR: So, what was decided?

COLONEL: It was agreed that Wolski would collect evidence of Popieluszko's activities which would convince the Church authorities to put pressure on the priest. At that meeting I formulated a view that Father Popieluszko could give up or, to be more realistic, curtail his politically harmful activities.

PROSECUTOR: Did you consider the use of physical force?

COLONEL: There were no recommendations to use physical force; for one main reason, which is not just an empty phrase. Because, brought up in the discipline of socialist humanism, we respect the principle that the political opponent should be fought with political, social arguments, and not with force or fists.

PROSECUTOR: Accused Piotrowski, what is your recollection of that meeting?

[PIOTROWSKI *rises in the dock*.]

PIOTROWSKI: Colonel Adam Pietruszka here said: 'Enough of this lark with Popieluszko and Malkowski. We are going to take resolute action. It is necessary to shake them up so much that it could cause a coronary. Simply, it is necessary to give them final warnings'. The Colonel chose Father Malkowski as the first for this kind of action and at the same time gave a typical example — I don't know if I mentioned this during the pre-trial investigation but I remembered it later — namely an example of how this action was to look. The best thing would be if somebody attacked Malkowski in a dark alley and gave him a thorough beating and, ideally, if two minutes later the police found the perpetrator, some kind of small-time crook.

PROSECUTOR: What was your reaction to this?

PIOTROWSKI: I said, more or less, knowing really well the activities of these two gentlemen, Malkowski and Popieluszko, I stated that Malkowski — I used this expression, sorry to say this — that Malkowski had brass lungs, he made a lot of noise, his bark was worse than his bite. Whereas Popieluszko had strong links and was much more dangerous politically. The Colonel suggested we present him with a plan of action. And then he said, 'I've got nothing to add, Comrades. But I can tell you this decision has been taken at the highest or, at least, a very high level'.

OLSZEWSKI: What did you think that meant?

PIOTROWSKI: A few days later, maybe September 25th, we were summoned to General Platek's office—

OLSZEWSKI: The Head of the Department?

PIOTROWSKI: Yes. We were to report on the general situation and on the illegal activities of five Warsaw priests. Those present at the meeting were Wolski, myself, General Platek, and the Colonel. The Colonel complained that Wolski was dragging his feet. Wolski explained he was making plans but had trouble with people, equipment, bosses. The Colonel said, 'Don't plan so much, do something'. He also said, 'You shouldn't worry so much about your superiors. If they know less, they won't get a headache'.

PROSECUTOR: Accused Piotrowski, what was your personal attitude to Father Popieluszko?

PIOTROWSKI: My attitude to Jerzy Popieluszko as a human being was, in fact, indifferent. I would even call it officially cool. My attitude to Jerzy Popieluszko, Your Honour, was in principle of no interest to me. I am a good-tempered man and it's difficult to upset me. Although I knew Jerzy Popieluszko hated the authorities, I was, as I say, indifferent to him. I never even spared him a thought after office hours. But he contravened the law and what irritated me was that the forces of law and order were powerless. When I saw that all other available forms and methods of work had failed, I must admit that I decided — I simply agreed — to undertake illegal action. In any case, it seemed to me there were times when a lesser evil was necessary to avert a greater evil. I do not say I have been a man without fault throughout his life. That wasn't the case. But I am convinced of one thing: that Pekala, Chmielewski, who are sitting in the dock with me here today, and myself would never have been in the dock if the law had been the law for Jerzy Popieluszko as well.

PROSECUTOR: How then did you proceed?

PIOTROWSKI: Esteemed Court, I want to say this: if I had shouted out in our Department asking who wanted to take part in the operation against Popieluszko, many would have volunteered. Today I am a hundred per cent sure that if someone had shouted: 'Those willing to damage Popieluszko — come forth!' I wouldn't have been able to complain about the shortage of volunteers among security service functionaries.

PROSECUTOR: But what did you do?

PIOTROWSKI: I came to the conclusion that it was a relatively dangerous task, demanding physical proficiency. I decided that action of this nature could only be carried out with Waldemar Chmielewski and Leszek Pekala, due to their physical suitability, and also due to the fact that they were workers whom I greatly trusted. They were good workers. Possibly on the same day, or the next day, I asked them to stay after 16.00 hours because I wanted to talk to them.

OFFICIAL: The accused, Leszek Pekala.

[PEKALA *rises in the dock.*]

PROSECUTOR: When did you become involved in this affair concerning Father Popieluszko?

PEKALA: A week or so before 13th October. Chief Piotrowski asked me for the first time to his office. He asked whether I would like to take part in a dangerous mission. I said, in principle, yes, but that I'd like to know what it was all about. Piotrowski said that Father Popieluszko was to be kidnapped. He said the superiors had given their go-ahead, even if loss of health and life was to be risked.

OLSZEWSKI: Loss of health and life?

PEKALA: At first, he mentioned only loss of health, but the next day he said that loss of life should also be considered and that he had the go-ahead for that as well.

PROSECUTOR: And what was your reaction to this?

PEKALA: I asked for time to think about it.

OLSZEWSKI: And then you agreed?

PEKALA: I felt it could be an important case in my life, that it might advance my future career. Piotrowski said he would be responsible to the 'top' for everything. The technical details were left to Chmielewski and me. I was to be responsible for driving the car. The Chief said we were to choose the place of kidnap. We were given a week off work. Chmielewski pretended to be ill. I got days off that were already due to me.

OLSZEWSKI: What did Piotrowski mean by 'the top'?

PEKALA: At first, no names of the bosses were mentioned at all. Later, he mentioned Pietruszka a number of times.

JUDGE: I want to quote from your pre-trial testimony. Quote, 'Piotrowski mentioned three names, but I do not want to name two of them since I'm not sure of the context in which they were mentioned', unquote. What did you mean by that?

PEKALA: By 'the top' I understood that Deputy Department Head Pietruszka had been acquainted with the case.

JUDGE: Let me quote something else from your pre-trial testimony. Quote, 'I understood that this decision had been approved at the level of Deputy Minister', unquote.

PEKALA: I do not confirm this. I stress that the driving force behind all actions was Chief Piotrowski.

JUDGE: Does the defendant Piotrowski agree with the implication that he was the leader of this group of people?

PIOTROWSKI: Esteemed Court: I would rather say, the stronger personality.

OLSZEWSKI: How did the accused hope to use the kidnapping of Father Popieluszko?

PIOTROWSKI: I did not envisage that he would suffer any injuries, but that he would simply disappear suddenly for a day. I had the concept — I would not like to expatiate at length here — this concept was based on the deceived husband, the revenge of the jealous husband. I had at my disposal knowledge which, if made proper use of during a talk, recorded on a cassette tape, could lead to Jerzy Popieluszko believing that this was a jealous husband really out for revenge. And I assumed that by making such a cassette I would be able to exert a certain pressure on Popieluszko, to bring him to end his activities.

PROSECUTOR: What does the idea based on the deceived husband mean? We do not understand this.

PIOTROWSKI: I simply had information about relations maintained by Jerzy Popieluszko with a certain lady. Should the need arise I can give the name and recount the circumstances, hotels, restaurants and so on. But I do not think it necessary. I wanted ordinarily, crudely, to blackmail Popieluszko.

COLONEL: May it please the Court, I knew Piotrowski had this type of evidence at his disposal, but later the person in question entered into marriage and so, for us, the institution of marriage, the stability of marriage, is a supreme value, and Piotrowski was instructed to destroy that evidence. In this case, that type of evidence was not to be utilized.

[*Light on* CHROSTOWSKI.]

CHROSTOWSKI: And so they discussed various plans to kidnap the priest, in order, they say, to make him give up his political activities and to disclose the names and whereabouts of underground activists. First, they think of holding him in a wartime bunker. Then, they think of taking him to a bridge on the Vistula River and hanging him over it. The ideas grow like mushrooms in the rain. Perhaps they should push him out of a train, or bury him in the ground up to his neck so that he dies from exposure. And then they decide to cause the accident on 13th October on the road from Gdansk. And when Pekala gets the keys of an official car, a Fiat 125P, Adam Pietruszka wishes him luck. It doesn't do him much good. But if I hadn't frightened off Piotrowski by driving at him, they meant to burn the car and its occupants. They bought twenty litres of petrol for the purpose.

[PIOTROWSKI *rises in the dock.*]

PIOTROWSKI: I have misled the esteemed Court with one of my statements. When I was asked about my attitude to Jerzy Popieluszko, I said it was professionally cool. It was not professionally cool. Esteemed Court, my attitude to the matter as a whole was somewhat different. My work, esteemed Court, involved me with all manifestations of violations of the rule of law by the Roman Catholic clergy. For instance — and let those in Court wearing the uniform of the police listen to me with particular attention — when one of their colleagues was murdered by Father Zych, who had been sentenced for his crime and was supposed to be transferred from prison to a monastery, so as not to be an upsetting sight — such an arrangement was forced upon the authorities by the Episcopate — and this priest-murderer even now celebrates Mass in a monastery, all because the rabble should not be upset. How can one keep calm when one knows that one of the bishops co-operated with the Gestapo during the war? How can one, Your Honour, stay calm when public praises are sung of how nice the Gestapo was during the war and that those Gestapo people were so smartly dressed, such clever people, so well-educated? How can one stay calm, Your Honour, when every year taxes due from the Church are waived? How could one stay calm, Your Honour, when schools were being occupied, thus flouting the law, and young people were incited? One could not stay calm, Your Honour, when during one of the street demonstrations in Gdansk a runner was caught carrying a miniature radio of the walkie-talkie type, and the radio direction measurements indicated where the central transmitter was: in the presbytery of the St. Brigida Church. It became impossible to remain calm in this situation. No free Saturdays, no free Sundays. Our children did not see their parents and all because a few priests felt like stirring up trouble. And all who give witness here, those who sit in the dock, not to mention the Prosecutor and Your Honour, would have an assigned place if that new rising of which Popieluszko spoke came about. I was not officially cool. That is all I wanted to say.

[OLSZEWSKI *rises*.]

OLSZEWSKI: Your Honour! The Court is admitting elements of political theatre and I express my concern. This is one of the most serious trials in Poland since the war. It is a trial for murder with political implications, a crime recognized as a political provocation —

PROSECUTOR: I have to protest against calling the deed committed by defendant Piotrowski a murder. Polish law does not provide for 'murder' but 'manslaughter'. Perhaps this word has been used after the weekly *Time* Magazine which was circulating yesterday in the Court's lobby.

OLSZEWSKI: It's not a question of terminology and although Article 148 of the Penal Code calls killing a man 'manslaughter', the concept of 'murder' is also used.

PIOTROWSKI: I would like to say a few words, too. I protest against such wording by the Auxiliary Prosecutor because I've never admitted to having killed Father Popieluszko. He did not die because he didn't agree with the realities of the State-Church relationship. It happened as a result of quite different circumstances.

OLSZEWSKI: We shall see.

[OLSZEWSKI *sits.*]

PROSECUTOR: Accused Piotrowski, you and your subordinates failed in your attempt to kidnap Father Popieluszko on 13th October. So, you decided to try again.

PIOTROWSKI: Esteemed Court, it has been stated that because the priest's car drove at me, on 13th October, that is, I was made to miss with the stone I threw. This is incorrect. I deliberately threw the stone above the car in which Popieluszko was travelling because I knew what the danger of hitting it would be. However, I went through the motions so as not to lose the confidence of my subordinates who might have thought I had wanted to withdraw from the action. You see, esteemed Court, we made so many errors because we were not professionals. On the Monday after that first attempt, Adam Pietruszka asked me to his office to report. I told him everything about the unsuccessful attempt with a stone. He said: 'Pity, it could have been such a beautiful accident'. I did not say I'd missed on purpose.

PROSECUTOR: Let us come to the events that culminated in the kidnapping of Father Popieluszko on 19th October, 1984. The priest had travelled to Bydgoszcz in order to take part in a Mass.

PIOTROWSKI: Yes. I told Adam Pietruszka that when we go to Bydgoszcz our action would be improved and more successful.

[*Light on* CHROSTOWSKI.]

CHROSTOWSKI: Once more, Pekala and Chmielewski are given days off to prepare. They steal number-plates which are going to be used later on. And they're given a 'W' Pass which exempts them from police road-blocks. And what else do they need for this journey? Pekala brings a T-shirt from home. Chmielewski borrows handcuffs from a colleague. He gets hold of a policeman's jacket with a sergeant's stripes, a white cap-cover — that's what the traffic boys wear — and an eagle badge. They set off for Bydgoszcz, a town about 250 kilometres north-west of Warsaw. And there is something else.

PROSECUTOR: Accused Pekala, can you say whether, before setting off for Bydgoszcz, there were two sacks of stones in the Fiat or one sack?

PEKALA: I think there were two.

PROSECUTOR: How were they got ready? You put the stones into the sacks, and the sacks were fastened in some way?

PEKALA: Yes, they were tied with some string I had.

PROSECUTOR: How many stones were there?

PEKALA: I can't say exactly but I think there were about ten of them.

JUDGE: Could the defendant express this in kilogrammes?

PEKALA: About thirty.

JUDGE: You got these stones and took them to your place of work?

PEKALA: Yes.

JUDGE: Who saw these stones? Did the defendant Piotrowski see them too, or was it just you and the defendant Chmielewski?

PEKALA: I don't know. They were kept in a cupboard in my office.

JUDGE: And then they were packed into sacks?

PEKALA: Yes.

PROSECUTOR: Why were there two sacks of stones? Why two?

PEKALA: Yes. They were got ready in case the priest was to be returning home with someone else and two people were to be kidnapped, frightened. Well, that's how I understood it.

PROSECUTOR: And what had the second person to do with it?

PEKALA: If a second person were to die, then — [He stops.]

PROSECUTOR: Is the accused saying, to die?

PEKALA: Yes.

PROSECUTOR: What am I to understand by, 'if a second person were to die'?

PEKALA: Were to be killed.

[Light on CHROSTOWSKI.]

CHROSTOWSKI: What you're to understand is that they're talking about me. Well, they set off for Bydgoszcz. On the way they fill up with petrol. When they get to the town they wait outside the church. They're in a Fiat, registration number WAB 6031. The registration number is important, because it's one belonging to the Ministry of the Interior, and the police in Bydgoszcz know that. In fact, one of the local policemen spots it. Later, he says, he sees what he thinks is another Fiat, only this time the number is KZC 0243, and he remembers that because the registration plates are unnaturally clean. What happened was that the three accused, realizing a Mass was still in progress, drive off to the outskirts of the town, and change the number belonging to the Ministry to the spanking clean KZC 0243 which, of course, they'd stolen. They return to the church and hear somebody discussing the KZC number. At that moment, Piotrowski was out of the car, seeing what was going on in the church. When he comes back, they tell him: 'Somebody's writing down our registration number'. 'Let 'em write it down', he says. He wasn't particularly bothered.

PROSECUTOR: Accused Pekala, by the time you arrived in Bydgoszcz you had posts with you. Where did you get them and who made them?

PEKALA: You're talking about the cudgels, aren't you? We got them on the way. We broke off some posts from a fence.

PROSECUTOR: What were they to be used for, these stakes, cudgels?

PEKALA: To stun the driver and the passenger. After we changed the number-plates, we wrapped two clubs in pieces of the T-shirt I'd brought from home.

[OLSZEWSKI *rises*.]

I'm very tired now. I'd like to rest.

JUDGE: Very well, the witness is excused for the moment.

[PEKALA *sits*.]

OFFICIAL: The witness, Waldemar Chrostowski.

[CHROSTOWSKI *takes the witness stand*.]

PROSECUTOR: When you were waiting for Father Popieluszko on 19th October, was anything happening in front of the presbytery at that time?

CHROSTOWSKI: I think that Father Jerzy said that a bright-coloured Fiat was in front of the presbytery and that the secret police were watching the presbytery.

PROSECUTOR: Why should he pay attention to this? Did cars not park there?

CHROSTOWSKI: It's not that they didn't park there, it's just that cars would park on that spot frequently, for a reason that is well known, to watch the presbytery. It was no secret to us at all, since these cars would change with each other in such a specific way, it would have been difficult not to notice it: they would roll up, flash their lights, one would leave, and one would arrive and park on the same spot.

OLSZEWSKI: Was that the time there was a conversation about coffee?

CHROSTOWSKI: Oh no, that's earlier. Between the 13th and the 19th.

OLSZEWSKI: Well then, tell us about that.

CHROSTOWSKI: Well, the Father noticed that one of these cars was parked and the weather was quite cold at that time. Two men were sitting inside. Father Jerzy says, 'Go up to these gentlemen', he says, 'they've been sitting here two or three hours already', he says, 'they're cold in the car, they're shivering', so, he says, 'maybe they'll want a drink of coffee, because we can arrange for that'. Well, I go up to them with one of my acquaintances, and I ask whether they'd like some coffee. He says, 'We know you're on duty'. They answered — in fact they were offended —

OLSZEWSKI: [*stimultaneously*] Offended?

CHROSTOWSKI: [*continuing*] — and they wouldn't drink any coffee, and the incident ended at that.

PROSECUTOR: So, on the 19th October, when it was already dark, after the Mass, you set off from Bydgoszcz for Warsaw in a Volkswagen Golf motor-car, with Father Jerzy Popieluszko as your passenger.

CHROSTOWSKI: Yes, we take this road, the Torun road. I'd covered maybe fifteen kilometres when I notice the lights of a car. I notice in my mirror that a car's coming up to us.

PROSECUTOR: What speed were you doing?

CHROSTOWSKI: At first, I really did step on it, because I want to get home as soon as possible, because it's night time, but Father Jerzy says slow down, he says, we'll get there, he says, and he says we'll always find time to be late. I slow down. I'm doing some 100 kilometres an hour, but then the other car begins to gain on us. I even say to the Father, I says, some nutcase is driving with his full beam on, I says, and I can't see anything, I says, he's blinding me all the time, I says. So, I fiddle with my mirror, and I step on it. I left that car behind. I left it behind for a kilometre maybe, and then I slow down again to maintain my previous speed. This happens maybe three times. In the end, I give up dodging him because he keeps the same distance all the time. He doesn't approach and he doesn't overtake. Just the opposite. As if he's trying to blind me. Maliciously. And in the end I decide to let him through to overtake me so that I can go on in peace. Then the car behind comes nearer, at quite high speed. He's already flashing his lights, several times. I turn the car more to the right, slow down even more, to seventy, sixty, maybe, to allow overtaking, as safe as possible. Then that car reaches me. It doesn't overtake me, but drives parallel with me and on the right I see an officer flashing a red light at me. I see a uniform. Father Popieluszko sees it too. He says, 'Slow down, we'll see what sort of check it is'. The Fiat overtakes us and stops on the right. I pass it but watch whether he's stopping us. And then I see a hand sticking out of the car. I see that officer who's waving the torch. He's wearing the uniform of a traffic policeman. Father Jerzy says then, 'Stop, otherwise we'll get into trouble'. I says, 'Listen, I can't stop in these circumstances, in the wood, it doesn't make sense to stop. Let's drive further, to a village'. 'Stop, stop', he says, 'because we'll be in trouble'. Then I see in the rear mirror that the officer's coming from the Fiat and approaching me.

OFFICIAL: The accused, Waldemar Chmielewski.

> [CHMIELEWSKI *rises. He is in a terrible state, trembling and twitching. When he speaks, he stammers from time to time.*]

PROSECUTOR: Tell us what was happening in the Fiat while you were following the Volkswagen Golf towards Torun.

CHMIELEWSKI: The chief said to Pekala: 'Turn on the headlights'.

PROSECUTOR: What was that supposed to mean?

CHMIELEWSKI: I don't know. I started changing into a uniform. I put on the uniform. I didn't know what to do with my hands so I tore off the eagle badge from the police cap and took off the cap-cover, putting it into a pocket. I had to do something with my hands because — because —

PROSECUTOR: From nervousness?

JUDGE: One moment. Have you a permanent speech impediment or has it been brought on by this situation?

CHMIELEWSKI: No, yes.

JUDGE: Pardon?

CHMIELEWSKI: This has appeared following all this —

[BARBARA MARCZUK, *the Defence Counsel, rises.*]

MARCZUK: Your Honour, the defendant has been examined by a doctor who has defined his condition as a speech impediment of nervous origin. The doctor proposes that he be permitted to testify sitting down.

JUDGE: So, the conclusion is that he is physically and psychologically fully capable of giving evidence.

MARCZUK: At the moment, yes.

JUDGE: Let the defendant, Chmielewski, be seated. Continue to interrogate him.

[CHMIELEWSKI *sits.*]

PROSECUTOR: What happened when the priest's car stopped?

CHMIELEWSKI: I got out of our car with Piotrowski. He was in civilian clothes. Pekala remained at the wheel. We approached the Golf from the driver's side. I said that we wanted to carry out a road-check.

CHROSTOWSKI: I heard the voice of the civilian. He almost shouted, 'The keys, the keys'. Then the officer said, 'Please give me the keys, because you'll have to be breathalysed, let's go to the car', he says, 'take out the keys'. I hesitated for a second. I had the feeling something was wrong. I'd never been asked for the keys by any officer before. At that moment the officer tore the keys from my grasp. He probably gave them to the civilian straight away, into his hand. The officer says, 'Driver, get out of the car. You will get into our car. You will be breathalysed'. So, I went towards the Fiat and got in to the front seat, beside the driver, thinking all the time that I'd be breathalysed.

CHMIELEWSKI: Piotrowski ordered me to guard the Golf car and he himself went with Chrostowski towards our car.

MARCZUK: Defendant Pekala, did the driver of the Volkswagen Golf get into your car without putting up any opposition?

PEKALA: Yes, he did. Piotrowski said to him a sentence to the effect that there would be a check or a sobriety test, and giving me the handcuffs he said, 'Please', or he even just said, 'Put the handcuffs on him'.

CHROSTOWSKI: I think to myself, why handcuffs? I was very much surprised. Handcuffs for a sobriety test? I knew something was starting to happen that wasn't right.

PEKALA: Then, Piotrowski said — he used the diminutive for Waldemar — 'Waldus', he said. 'Open your mouth', and stuffed a piece of rag in his mouth.

CHROSTOWSKI: He tried to stuff the rag in fairly far but I controlled it with my tongue.

PEKALA: Piotrowski got out. He said, in a specially loud voice, probably so that Chrostowski would hear: 'Here you are. Here's a pistol. Be careful, it's cocked. Watch out, in case he wants to escape'.

PROSECUTOR: Did Chrostowski have a rattle in his throat after the gag was put in place?

PEKALA: At the beginning, no. A moment later only. After Piotrowski had gone, I turned the radio on, so that I wouldn't hear it.

CHROSTOWSKI: I was just playing a game. It was a game on my part. I did the rattle on purpose.

PROSECUTOR: [*to* PEKALA] Did Piotrowski, getting out of the car, take a baton with him?

PEKALA: I can't answer that question.

PROSECUTOR: And Chmielewski, when he got out, did he take a baton with him?

PEKALA: I didn't see. Both of them were on the priest's side of the Golf, the passenger side.

CHMIELEWSKI: I was sitting in the car, beside the priest. I received an instruction from Piotrowski. I conveyed it to the priest. It was a question of getting the priest to leave the car. I was disorientated and upset, among other things because it was the first time I had stopped people whilst wearing a uniform. Father Popieluszko asked me what was the matter. Piotrowski said it was a matter of checking identity. The priest was reluctant to leave the car. Piotrowski grabbed the door-handle. Then, the priest got out and he and Piotrowski went in the direction of our car. Piotrowski had ordered me to switch off the Golf's lights. I couldn't switch them off. I kept trying various switches. I wanted to get out but I couldn't find the door-handle. Finally, I opened the window and that was how I managed to open the door. I heard Piotrowski shouting, 'Waldek, come over here, he doesn't want to get in'. I asked the Reverend Popieluszko why he didn't want to get in. Then

I heard his reply: 'Because this man is dragging me off somewhere'.

OLSZEWSKI: Didn't it surprise you that they were at the back of the car? If they were supposed to have been getting into the car, why did they go to the back?

[CHMIELEWSKI *stammers and stutters unintelligibly.*]

The back of the car means the boot, is that right?

CHMIELEWSKI: Yes, I hadn't thought about that, Your Honour, I only saw the priest got pulled by Piotrowski—

PROSECUTOR: Which way was he pulled? Forwards? Backwards?

CHMIELEWSKI: Kind of behind the boot. Piotrowski was hitting the priest with a club which he held in his hand.

OLSZEWSKI: Did he hit him more than once?

CHMIELEWSKI: Certainly more than once.

OLSZEWSKI: Did these blows fell the priest to the ground?

CHMIELEWSKI: He was in the process of falling down when he was shaken. He was lying on his back. Piotrowski wanted to raise him. The Reverend was then, how shall I put it, somehow limp.

OLSZEWSKI: [*to* PEKALA] Did you hear any blows?

PEKALA: Just one for certain.

CHROSTOWSKI: I hear a dull sort of thud, just as if somebody's struck a bag of flour with a club or something. I also notice, out of the corner of my eye, the reaction of the driver: a kind of grimace, revulsion, contraction of his face somehow, it's difficult for me to define it, but something of this sort. I realize then that Father Popieluszko has been hit with some implement and that the driver's reaction confirmed it. At that moment I saw this shadow of a chance to save the whole situation and I gathered that from the driver's reaction. I notice that the driver had a vestige of humanity in him, of human reactions, quite simply — that something evil took place, and this was how he reacted, with such revulsion.

PIOTROWSKI: I hit the priest in a fit of blind rage. I struck Popieluszko several times because he wouldn't get into our car voluntarily—

CHROSTOWSKI: I was already aware that this was a common attack by bandits and that there was simply no point in entering into discussions with these gentlemen, but to deal with them as you would deal with bandits. I realized that only calm could

save me in this sort of situation. To struggle? I had no chance.
I was handcuffed and gagged.

CHMIELEWSKI: Piotrowski instructed me to get ropes from the car.
To tie the Reverend up. I passed the rope to Piotrowski. I
myself took things out of the boot and put them in the car.
Bags and sacks. I don't think the Reverend was gagged.

CHROSTOWSKI: I hear nothing for a bit. Then it sounds as if
someone's throwing something heavy into a chest.

PEKALA: A fairly heavy load was being put into the boot. I understood that to be probably the stunned priest—

CHROSTOWSKI: The civilian and the officer jump into the back of
the car, fast. One of them says: 'Go, step on it, put your foot
down'.

PEKALA: I was doing about eighty.

CHROSTOWSKI: After going two or three hundred metres, one of
the individuals in the back puts a rope on me. He simply says
to me, he says: 'Here you are, son, a little bit of rope for you, to
keep your gob shut on your last journey'.

PROSECUTOR: On what part of the body was the rope being put?

CHROSTOWSKI: On my mouth, so that it would push the gag in.
And he ties it at the back, round my head. Oh, I omitted to
mention one fact: the driver handed the pistol to those who
were sitting in the back. 'Give me the shooter', one of them
says. After that, I felt as though a barrel touched the back of
my head and I hear the order: 'Sit still', something like that.
The civilian then orders the driver to turn off the road. He
became angry when the driver didn't do it. He wanted him to
turn off into the forest, to find a clearing. I realized the situation wasn't funny. I knew these could be my last hours. My
first instinct was to grab the steering wheel as soon as we
speeded up, to cause an accident and overturn the car. But I
quickly gave up that idea because I realized that, if the priest
was lying in the boot, unconscious, he would never come out
alive from such an accident. I decide then that I have to jump
out of the car, but it has to be done where someone can see it,
because I know that after jumping I could become nothing
but a shadow, and I was determined to leave some sort of
trace, so that someone would react. I lean forward on the seat.
I feel the door-handle with my little finger. Then, we overtake
a small Fiat, and I also see, on the left side of the road, two
men standing near a motorcycle. I decide to jump in the light

of the small Fiat's headlamps, so that he'd see exactly what's going on. Simultaneously, I pull the door-handle, shove my shoulder against the door and open it. Hitting the ground wasn't much fun. I curled up and let my body roll.

PROSECUTOR: Was it your first jump of this kind, did you train for something like that?

CHROSTOWSKI: I'm a fireman, and I did my national service in the airborne division.

PROSECUTOR: So what happened after you hit the road?

CHROSTOWSKI: The moment I could, I jumped to my feet. Of course, then I didn't feel pain. I realized the handcuffs were unfastened. I tried to stop the small Fiat. The reaction of the driver was shocking to me. He swerves to the left, passes me, and drives away. I remember the two men beside the motorcycle. I tell them briefly what's happened. I ask them to follow the Fiat. They say the motorcycle's broken and can't be used. I look round and see a large building with lights on. I run towards it, not knowing what kind of building it is.

PROSECUTOR: What were the instructions after Chrostowski's escape?

PEKALA: The instructions were: go on, go on. I was directed to the right and to the left, and in that way we arrived at the Vistula, to a sort of piece of open ground. I was given the instruction to open the boot-lid. Then, I noticed the priest running, Father Popieluszko was running away. Piotrowski shouted, 'Get him!' But he was the first to reach the priest—

PROSECUTOR: Was Father Popieluszko behaving calmly, was he quiet, or did he call out, did he shout?

PEKALA: He was calling for help, shouting: 'People, help. Spare my life'. I couldn't see clearly but then I think Piotrowski hit him and the priest fell down.

PIOTROWSKI: I want to add that any blow inflicted on Father Popieluszko was not once a beating for beating's sake. Popieluszko would not have received a single blow if everything had gone according to plan.

PROSECUTOR: [to PEKALA] What did he hit him with?

PEKALA: I think it was a club.

PROSECUTOR: Did he already have a club in his hand?

PEKALA: Throughout the whole event, right to the end, I see a club in Piotrowski's hands, so it's difficult for me to say—

PIOTROWSKI: I beat him unconscious with my fists, hitting him on the back of the head. Because when the priest's driver jumped out of the car, I lost control. It was the first time in my life as an adult that I'd hit another person.

PROSECUTOR: [*to* PEKALA] At that point, did you put sticking-plaster on his mouth?

PEKALA: No.

PROSECUTOR: When you put Father Popieluszko back in the boot was he conscious or unconscious?

PEKALA: Unconscious.

PIOTROWSKI: When the boot-lid was shut we set out in the direction of Wloclawek, we continued to drive very slowly, the car was loaded down, we were unable to reach a speed higher than 50-60 kilometres per hour.

CHROSTOWSKI: By then I must have reached the building with its lights on. I ran up the staircase. I didn't see anyone downstairs so I went upstairs and ran into a room where there was a group of men and I begin explaining what's happened, that I need a telephone. Those gentlemen take me downstairs to the doorkeeper's room. There was a lady there. I explain to her what's happened, that the priest's been kidnapped, and that I must contact Warsaw immediately. I wanted to ring the Curia or the Episcopate. The lady's unable to get a connection, so I ask her to ring the nearest church in the neighbourhood, and I ask her to ring for an ambulance because I was beginning to feel the effects of the fall, and she informed the police.

PIOTROWSKI: I was a hundred per cent certain of pursuit, so I said aloud to turn off the road and proceed towards Lodz—

PEKALA: The priest began to move inside the boot. I can't remember who got the idea, who simply realized we should stop at a petrol station and buy oil.

CHMIELEWSKI: When Piotrowski went to buy the oil, we got out of the car and I noticed there was something big bulging from the boot. I tried to press the boot-lid down with my hands. But then I jumped on and pressed down — may the Court pardon the expression — with my buttocks.

PEKALA: When we left the petrol station, we'd gone about five hundred metres and turned off the road to the right, into a thicket, bushes of some sort—

PROSECUTOR: During this time, was Father Popieluszko moving inside the boot? Was he trying to prise the boot-lid open?

[*The lights, almost imperceptibly, begin to concentrate entirely on the dock so that it becomes the only focus of attention.*]

PEKALA: I was instructed to drive very slowly, and they were running at the back of the car and holding down the boot-lid. I was told to stop the car. The priest was beaten, still inside the boot. I think the priest was beaten by Piotrowski with a club. He was moving and I think Piotrowski hit him again. The priest was moving, perhaps, but it was all kind of torpid. That was when the bindings on his hands and legs, as well as the gag on his mouth, were tightened.

OLSZEWSKI: Who was doing the gagging? Who was putting the gag on? Who was adjusting it?

PEKALA: Myself on his hands and with somebody's assistance around his head. Piotrowski said at least once that if he didn't stay quiet, he would kill him.

OLSZEWSKI: How did he say that?

PEKALA: 'I will strangle him with my own hands'. Afterwards we drove off.

PIOTROWSKI: It was then difficult to think logically at all. There was a moment when Chmielewski said that Popieluszko was moving in the boot—

CHMIELEWSKI: I saw the priest's face. The light in the boot was on. I saw his face.

PIOTROWSKI: I leaned out and I, too, saw his face. I was amazed. Immediately I sat back. I thought perhaps I was dreaming. I don't know why the light was on in the boot, but I remember that through a wide gap in the lid I saw the face of Popieluszko; it seemed to me that it was the face of a dead man. I have seen many dead people, for example, my mother, I'd been to resuscitation wards in hospitals, and I was sure Popieluszko was dead.

CHMIELEWSKI: Piotrowski told Pekala to stop the car. We all got out. Then I saw Piotrowski with a gun in his hand, saying, 'If you move, I'll shoot you'. I was standing stupidly in the road and couldn't take my eyes off the Reverend. I was paralysed. Piotrowski was fixing something with the gag. He screamed, 'Must I do everything myself, then?' Pekala suggested he should grab the priest by the nose because he had some problem pushing the gag in. I saw Piotrowski do that and I think he managed to push the gag in. The Reverend didn't move. We shut him in the boot.

PEKALA: Piotrowski instructed us to look for a wood. We were wondering whether to free the priest there.

PIOTROWSKI: What was to be done? Was he to be left, presumed dead, somewhere in a ditch by the side of the road? In any case, we drove on. We arrived at a road junction. A police patrol was visible from a distance. A policeman came out of the patrol car. At the signal to stop I leant over and showed the 'W' pass through the window. The policeman waved us on. I told Pekala to turn back. We'll go via the dam.

PEKALA: After a few minutes we turned into the wood. Some three hundred metres. We got out. The priest was removed from the boot. Piotrowski gave the order to tie stones to his legs. Yes, he used the phrase: 'Stones to the legs'. He was talking about water.

PROSECUTOR: When you tied those stones to his legs, did Father Popieluszko show any signs of life?

PEKALA: Definitely not.

PROSECUTOR: You tied the sack full of stones, and what happened next?

PEKALA: Yes, I put a loop around his neck and then the knot round his legs—

PROSECUTOR: Was it the defendant's own idea to tie him up in this way?

PEKALA: If you mean the noose, yes.

OLSZEWSKI: Did that noose work so that if the priest tried to stretch his legs, he would at the same time strangle?

PEKALA: It would strangle, yes.

PROSECUTOR: What happened to the gag? Was his mouth fully covered with the sticking-plaster?

PEKALA: The mouth was covered.

PROSECUTOR: Was any decision made then, a final decision about what to do next?

PEKALA: Both Chmielewski and I tried to convince Piotrowski that this was nonsense, that it was impossible for the priest to die. He was battered and surely so scared that, if he survived, he would surely stop acting in this manner. It was certainly then that Piotrowski used the expression that water was the only thing, that the priest had to disappear.

PROSECUTOR: How did you react to that?

PEKALA: I felt powerless, as if hemmed in. I stopped thinking logically. I could not see how it even could have reached that stage. But I knew that I had to obey.

OLSZEWSKI: You did not have to.

PEKALA: Now I know I did not.

CHMIELEWSKI: There were two road checks, one soon after the other, not far apart—

OLSZEWSKI: Did you make use of the 'W' pass in both instances?

CHMIELEWSKI: Yes.

OLSZEWSKI: And no checks of any kind took place?

CHMIELEWSKI: No.

OLSZEWSKI: Father Popieluszko was still in the boot. If a thorough check was made at the time, the fact would have come to light, wouldn't it?

CHMIELEWSKI: Certainly.

OLSZEWSKI: Was the pass, therefore, of great significance to you?

CHMIELEWSKI: Certainly.

PIOTROWSKI: We turned right on to the dam. We crossed the dam. We stopped the car by the outlet. I said, 'We have to get rid of him here'. The three of us got out of the car.

PROSECUTOR: [*to* PEKALA] Did you check on whether the priest was alive or dead?

PEKALA: I don't know because I was the third to approach him, but I got the impression that the priest was rather dead.

PIOTROWSKI: We took the body of Father Jerzy Popieluszko and we drowned it.

CHMIELEWSI: The body went in vertically. We simply shifted it over the railings and, after a moment, let it go, together, as it were. No special signal was given. I remember I heard a loud splash.

PIOTROWSKI: We left the vicinity of the dam. We went back the way we had come. I can't describe the atmosphere in the car. I was horror-struck because what had happened was not what had been planned. I tried to cheer them up.

CHMIELEWSKI: Piotrowski was saying, 'Don't worry, they won't find him'. And even if we're asked about it, we simply say we know nothing. He said nobody would be permitted to interrogate us, or even to take our fingerprints.

PIOTROWSKI: We were supposed to have those guarantees, after all. There were supposed to have been agreements to give us protection, when it had come to death. I thought that if anything happened they would probably rescue us. If anything happened, maybe they would send us abroad. Pekala said that that would suit him fine. There was a general feeling of dread.

CHMIELEWSKI: Piotrowski kept reassuring us we should never admit, even if we sometimes had to talk on the subject, never to admit where the body was. I cannot explain it rationally, but I simply didn't know what to do, and those words that as long as the body wasn't found, well, it was horrible, but, I don't know, they were some kind — well, I knew that I had to carry on obeying Piotrowski.

PIOTROWSKI: There came a moment when Pekala said he just had to have a drink of vodka. The alcohol was not drunk, esteemed Court, to celebrate anything. It was a rapid drinking of alcohol in order to have something to do.

CHMIELEWSKI: I know that all the time I kept throwing out different things, whatever I could lay my hands on: ropes, rags, stones, a vodka bottle. I was doing that all the time, I can't explain why. Piotrowski said he would take everything upon himself, and at the same time, he used the expression that forensic science is in our pocket, forensic science is ours, that it is ours, that we shouldn't worry.

[*He stands shivering and trembling.*]

[*The lights fade.*]

END OF ACT ONE

ACT TWO

On the screen: FATHER POPIELUSZKO's *body being recovered from the Vistula. It is laid on the bank.*

VOICE: The body is lying prostrate, soiled all over; the face bears traces of beating and is blood-stained; the cassock is raised above the hip-level; the legs are tied together; the arms, too, bear traces of tying up; a weighted jute sack is tied to the legs. A clerical collar can now be seen round the neck, and there are documents in the pocket. Can you please take out the documents, open them and read out the surname.

SHADOWY FIGURE: [*reading, with difficulty*] Jerzy Aleksander, Okapy, Dabrowa district.

VOICE: Is the surname illegible?

SHADOWY FIGURE: Popieluszko.

VOICE: Thank you. The body will be wrapped in polythene, sealed and conveyed to a Forensic Medicine Institute for a further detailed examination as well as an autopsy. Thank you.

[*Light on* CHROSTOWSKI.]

CHROSTOWSKI: The body of the priest will, in time, also bear witness. Meanwhile, there are mysteries to be solved. Like, what happened to all those promises? 'Don't worry, they won't find him', and 'Nobody'll be allowed to question us, or even take our fingerprints'? Why was Piotrowski so certain? Was it really because someone higher up had given him assurances? Or were there other reasons? And the strangest thing of all, what happened to their agreement never to tell anyone where the body was? Because, when you think about it, there were only three people in the whole world who knew the exact spot where the priest had been thrown into the water. What happened, then, to make them talk? Why was the body of the priest ever found at all?

[*Light grows on the Court.*]

PROSECUTOR: Witness Chrostowski–

[CHROSTOWSKI *takes the stand.*]

Let me remind the Court that you had raised the alarm. You had come to a house. You persuaded a lady to telephone a

church and to send for an ambulance because you were beginning to feel the effects of your escape from the moving car—

CHROSTOWSKI: I was also saying to her to telephone the police.

PROSECUTOR: Quite so. Then, what?

CHROSTOWSKI: Soon, the ambulance arrives. The doctor wants to
see to my injuries then and there, but I ask him to inform any
church, and the police as soon as possible. Then, I'm taken to
an ambulance service station. I'm X-rayed, and my wounds
are dressed. A large group of policemen arrive, and interroga-
tion begins while my wounds are being dressed. They say I
should go to the Ministry of the Interior clinic. I agree. When
I get there, in the early hours of the morning, I say I'm feeling
fine and there's no need for me to stay. I didn't know what was
going on. After all, I thought I'd been stopped by police. I
wasn't sure of anybody. I didn't trust the police. The doctor
who looked after me was very kind. I was to be released on the
night of 20th October—

PROSECUTOR: In other words, twenty-four hours after the kidnapping occurred?

CHROSTOWSKI: Yes, but in fact I'm detained for another three
days. I'm worried something's wrong. But when I write a
complaint to the Prosecutor I get the true answer: they're
keeping me there for my own safety.

PROSECUTOR: When were you released?

CHROSTOWSKI: On 23rd October. A commando brigade escorts
me in two cars to the parish of St. Stanislaw Kostka — that's
Father Popieluszko's parish — where I live.

PROSECUTOR: Because you had been stopped by a policeman, you
didn't trust the police. This delayed the prosecuting organs
in their work.

CHROSTOWSKI: You're too right, I didn't trust the police. Perhaps
it wasn't justified. But I know the lady, the receptionist,
called the police straight away. So there was no delay on that
count.

PROSECUTOR: Has the witness ever been convicted for active re-
sistance against the police?

OLSZEWSKI: What is the purpose of that question? Witness Chrostowski is the chief witness for the indictment, called by the
Prosecutor himself. I do not understand, therefore, why the
Prosecutor wishes to undermine the credibility of the witness
he has himself summoned. I do hope that other witnesses will
be questioned with equal vigour.

PROSECUTOR: There are no 'our' and 'your' witnesses. We are all searching together for the objective truth in this trial.

CHROSTOWSKI: I'll answer the question. Yes, I was charged twice with assaulting the police. But I received suspended sentences. I would also like to say that it was me who was provoked. They assaulted me first.

[*The* PROSECUTOR *nods curtly, and* CHROSTOWSKI *leaves the stand, resuming his position as observer.*]

PROSECUTOR: Accused Piotrowski, on Saturday, 20th October, the morning after the kidnapping, while the last witness, Chrostowski, was under police protection, what did you do?

PIOTROWSKI: I went to work. I even got there a little early and I was startled when General Platek telephoned.

OLSZEWSKI: General Platek is Head of the Department?

PIOTROWSKI: Yes. His first question was: 'Do you know what happened to Popieluszko?' I understood at once that the Department had been alerted. I said I knew nothing. The General summoned me to his office. I found Adam Pietruszka there and another deputy-director. The General repeated his question. Again, I said I knew nothing. I looked at Adam Pietruszka who was sitting there quietly. I thought: until I talk to him, I know nothing. I was trying to remain calm. I was asked whether anyone had gone out of Warsaw or had taken a car. I said no. This conversation lasted an hour. The telephones were ringing all the time. As soon as I got back to my office, Adam Pietruszka phoned. I went to him and returned the 'W' pass, I put it down on his desk, I think. Then he asked: 'What? How?' I said I couldn't tell whether Popieluszko was alive.

COLONEL: And on the Sunday, esteemed Court, yet again Piotrowski had no information about what had happened to the priest. Piotrowski said that the questions even bored him. And, on the Sunday, he said this: 'Everyone keeps asking me, boss, I don't know, perhaps he's floating in the Vistula'. And with a shrug of his shoulders he left me. It shocked me, but it was so inconceivable that a security functionary should throw the priest into the water that I didn't admit the thought. To me it seemed absurd. It was based on blind faith combined with irrationality.

OLSZEWSKI: Can you please say what you did with this piece of news? After all, the whole apparatus of the Security Service and the entire police were put on the alert to find Father Popieluszko, dead or alive. You had this piece of news. What did you do with it?

COLONEL: I didn't do anything with this piece of news, apart from being shocked, as I said before.

OLSZEWSKI: Do you admit you were a Security Service Officer whose duty it was to find Father Popieluszko's kidnappers?

COLONEL: Yes, of course.

OLSZEWSKI: Were you appointed a member of a commission, or an operational group, which had been entrusted with this task in particular?

COLONEL: Yes, I was appointed a member of such a group.

OLSZEWSKI: Were you fully aware of the fact that your actions should be aimed at finding the kidnappers?

COLONEL: My actions, my—

OLSZEWSKI: I just want to know whether you fully realized what your duties were.

COLONEL: I fully realized what they were and I fully intended to find the kidnappers.

OLSZEWSKI: In that case, shouldn't you have followed up any lead that might have resulted in catching the perpetrators of the act?

COLONEL: I should have followed up each lead, but also on the basis, I don't really know on what basis, I decisively rejected—

OLSZEWSKI: Were you authorized to check the news about the priest's kidnapping, the news you were receiving, you alone, without passing them on to people who were also authorized to check them?

COLONEL: I didn't consider it to be checking, I considered it to be a rejection on the basis that it was nonsensical.

OLSZEWSKI: Were you authorized to assess what was absurd or not absurd?

COLONEL: The way I understood it at the time, yes.

PIOTROWSKI: The Colonel asked whether Popieluszko could be recovered. I said it wasn't up to me. There were many such conversations with the Colonel and with General Platek. I did not relate the whole story to the Colonel. We had sham conversations, even though both of us knew what was what. He was interested in only one thing: had we left any traces?

CHMIELEWSKI: I got home about four a.m. That was on Saturday,

20th October. Then a driver came and told me I had to report to work. Some documents or other were needed. I was in the Ministry after ten o'clock. I didn't find Piotrowski there. I felt ill. I went to the doctor. He called an ambulance. It took me to the polyclinic. High blood pressure and debility was diagnosed. I phoned Piotrowski. He said I should come because it was an important matter. He said the priest's driver, Chrostowski, had been detained and was giving vague explanations. He informed me about the conduct of the case. Piotrowski told me not to worry.

JUDGE: Where did Piotrowski get that information?

CHMIELEWSKI: I don't know exactly. I guessed it was from the bosses. Pekala arrived. Piotrowski acquainted him with the situation. He also said we mustn't meet in his office because it might be under surveillance, that it was bugged, that he'd had a note from the Colonel saying that the rooms might be under surveillance.

PIOTROWSKI: On Sunday morning, the Colonel said to me that it was necessary to begin a cover-up. I suggested, perhaps, to demand a ransom. He liked the idea. So we carried it out. But I would like to avail myself of the right to refuse to testify on this matter, because it was all quite idiotic.

PEKALA: I talked to Piotrowski on Sunday, 21st October, in the evening, in my private car. We were drinking beer. He then spoke, among other things, about actions to spread disinformation and my departure to Poznan in order to despatch from there an anonymous message.

CHMIELEWSKI: The idea was to telephone — [*becoming incoherent*] — that Father Popieluszko — send anonymous letters — [*trying to regain control*] — demanding a ransom for the priest and such-like. I had the impression I was being followed. I got more and more frightened. I told Piotrowski about this. He ordered me to go home and calm down.

[*The* PROSECUTOR *hands a paper to the* COURT OFFICIAL.]

OFFICIAL: The witness, Barbara Story.

[BARBARA STORY, *late twenties, takes the witness stand.*]

PROSECUTOR: You were Piotrowski's secretary?

STORY: Yes.

PROSECUTOR: Do you remember Friday, 19th October?

STORY: More or less. I had a call from General Platek. He asked: 'Is

Piotrowski in?' I said he wasn't, but that Colonel Pietruszka knew the reasons for his absence. At the end of the day, General Platek telephoned again and asked: 'Has Piotrowski come back yet?' I said that unfortunately he hadn't. And then I went home.

PROSECUTOR: And you returned to work on Monday.

STORY: On Monday.

PROSECUTOR: Do you remember what was going on in the Department?

STORY: I started my routine as usual. Chief Piotrowski came to the secretariat to see me. He gave me a piece of paper with a telephone number on it, and he gave me an order. I was to go out of the building and, using a public call box, make a phone call to the number on the piece of paper and give them information. He said it was the number of the duty officer of Police Central Command.

PROSECUTOR: What was the information you had to convey?

STORY: That on Friday, 19th, late evening, I was with my husband in the region of Torun, picking mushrooms. Our car broke down. We tried to stop some other car to get help and at one point a car came, a Fiat, light-coloured, which slowed down as if to stop, and then accelerated and went away. In addition, I had to give the registration number of the car, and say that the individuals in the car had had their descriptions published by the mass media.

PROSECUTOR: And what happened on Tuesday, 23rd October?

STORY: We received instructions to write statements about what we did on the 19th.

PROSECUTOR: You handed your written statement to Pietruszka's deputy. Did the deputy read it?

STORY: Not in my presence. On leaving, he said he was going to see the Colonel. In a very short time he returned and instructed me to alter the statement. On seeing my hesitation, he said: 'It's not my idea, it's an order from the Colonel'. He then rang up Pietruszka and held the ear-piece in such a way that I was able to hear snippets of conversation. Pietruszka's voice was so excited that no discussion was possible, and particularly with a secretary, this was completely out, in any case, he ordered that all details be taken out because they were unnecessary.

COLONEL: Esteemed Court: my deputy came and said that

secretary Story had remembered so many details that he was
somewhat doubtful she really could have remembered it all.
So I told him: the shorter the report the better. It is obvious
that, had I ordered anything to be changed in front of a
witness, it would be possible to say that our Department was
nothing more than a den of thieves. It's evident nonsense.

JUDGE: Had the defendant the right to interfere in the contents of
reports written by employees?

COLONEL: In my view, it did not follow that I interfered in the
contents of the reports. In my opinion, I had the duty to inter-
vene in the doubtful truth.

OLSZEWSKI: [*to* STORY] I understand that after Pietruszka's inter-
vention your statement was drastically shortened. Could you
please say whether the fact that General Platek telephoned
twice on the 19th was also deleted?

STORY: I included all that in the original statement.

OLSZEWSKI: But I am interested in what was left out.

STORY: As far as I remember, the idea was to cut it down, to leave
out all the details.

OLSZEWSKI: What did you think about Piotrowski's order to leave
the building, go to a public telephone booth and telephone
the police — was it normal in your work, in the line of duty?

STORY: I was not in the habit of disputing orders given to me.

OLSZEWSKI: Perhaps you could tell us this: did you often carry out
instructions to give false information?

JUDGE: But it turned out afterwards that this was disinformation.

OLSZEWSKI: I'm sorry. I don't understand that remark of the pre-
siding judge. [*to* STORY] Wasn't it disinformation that you
went to pick mushrooms in Torun?

STORY: No, I didn't go to pick mushrooms. That was untrue.

OLSZEWSKI: Are you of the opinion that you had to carry out every
instruction to give false information?

STORY: I don't know whether it was disinformation or not. It's my
duty to carry out orders.

OLSZEWSKI: On Saturday, October 20th, you already knew the
priest had been kidnapped. On Monday the 22nd, you
telephone Police Headquarters with false information. On
Tuesday 23rd, you are asked to write what you did on the
previous Friday. Didn't it all seem strange to you? Did you
report it to anyone?

STORY: Yes, but it was, I think, on the morning of the 25th,

Thursday the 25th. The day before I had been questioned all day long by the investigating officer. So, on the 25th, I went to General Platek and told him everything.

OLSZEWSKI: Why didn't you say what you knew to the investigating officer?

STORY: [*becoming flustered*] They asked me many questions. I didn't know what it was all about—

OLSZEWSKI: But you had important information concerning the kidnapping of Father Popieluszko.

STORY: I didn't know then that it was important.

OLSZEWSKI: So, on the 25th, you went to General Platek and told him all about it. Yes?

STORY: Yes, I reported to General Platek. I told him about the altered statements because I thought that if the Deputy Director gives instructions to change statements, then surely the Director himself must know something about it.

OLSZEWSKI: What I can't understand is why you didn't tell the investigative officer all this.

STORY: It must have been because I was very nervous. I was very upset, very agitated. I became ill I was so worried. [*She begins to cry.*] I am unable to think clearly.

OLSZEWSKI: Didn't you think that the information you had was important to the prosecuting organs?

STORY : I don't know the regulations of the Penal Code.

OLSZEWSKI: Were you a friend of Piotrowski's?

STORY: Yes.

OLSZEWSKI: Then perhaps you wanted for purely human reasons to protect him.

STORY: We used to meet socially and, knowing him and his wife, I didn't admit the thought that he could do a thing like this.

JUDGE: You weren't afraid of General Platek, but you were afraid of Colonel Pietruszka. What were you afraid of and why?

STORY: Both were very temperamental and impulsive. But General Platek was more humane, which I can't say for Pietruszka who was very spiteful and vindictive.

JUDGE: You didn't like Pietruszka?

STORY: I was afraid of him.

PROSECUTOR: Thank you.

[*She rises and goes. The* PROSECUTOR *hands a document to the* COURT OFFICIAL.]

OFFICIAL: Witness General Zenon Platek.

> [PLATEK *enters. In his late fifties, he is confident and relaxed.*]

PROSECUTOR: You are Director of the Department of the Interior Ministry in which the four accused served?

PLATEK: Yes.

PROSECUTOR: When did you first learn about this case?

PLATEK: You must understand that, before this case, Father Popieluszko was, to me, a marginal matter. I received the first news on Saturday, 20th October, at my private flat on the service telephone, from the chief of the unit here in Torun. As was my duty, I gave certain specific orders: to detain Mr. Waldemar Chrostowski so that he could explain in detail all the circumstances. For a doctor to look after him. No permission to allow anyone to see him, including even people from the Ministry, just the specially selected people, as he was the only witness and all sorts of things can happen. The next order was to make the car used by Chrostowski and Father Popieluszko secure and to start the search, to comb the woods. Following my arrival at the office, I called in Colonel Pietruszka and the deputies and I asked them: Does anyone have any information on this matter? None of them knew anything about it. Then I called in Piotrowski, whose responsibilities included these matters, and I asked him if someone from the Department, or perhaps he, had gone to Bydgoszcz. His reply was unambiguous: 'Nobody went, I did not go either'. Next, I ordered that two senior officers, two Colonels, in fact, be sent immediately to the Bydgoszcz and Torun area.

PROSECUTOR: Did you have any contacts with Church leaders?

PLATEK: I suggested to my superior, Minister Kiszczak, that the church leadership be informed. In fact, during the day I spoke to three bishops. One of them insisted that Mr. Chrostowski be released. I refused. I gave my reasons here: he was the only witness and he was unwell. I said bluntly: 'Without protection — well, anything could happen and that would be another disaster'.

PROSECUTOR: We're still talking about Saturday, 20th October, aren't we?

PLATEK: Yes. A communiqué was prepared. This was particularly important because we wanted to get the whole community involved. At home, I took sleeping pills and went to bed. Well, that didn't last long. There was a 'phone call from my Colonel in Bydgoszcz. Nothing special to report, apart from a car with the registration KZC 0243. He also said that a car was seen in Bydgoszcz with Warsaw registration plates, on Friday the 19th, and in it there were three men. The car probably had a registration number WAB. The following morning, Sunday 21st, I arrived at the Ministry. I saw a car with the registration number WAB 6031. I called in Colonel Pietruszka, told him I'd seen the car. I said: 'Please clarify if this car was taken out into the field'.

COLONEL: General Platek said: 'Listen, driving through the parking lot I saw a car with the number-plates WAB 6031, the numbers seen in Bydgoszcz. They're from Piotrowski's section. Call Piotrowski, do something about it, don't let it stand there and be so noticeable, until the case is sorted out'. I didn't take it as an attempt at deception. In my opinion, I thought it could mean: 'Let Piotrowski know about it'. I said to Piotrowski, 'Listen, Comrade Piotrowski, your number-plates have been noted down in Bydgoszcz'. After thirty minutes, Piotrowski reported to me that he had changed the operational number-plates for official registration numbers.

OLSZEWSKI: The accused learns from General Platek that the car is in the Ministry's car-park and General Platek tells him: 'Do something about it so that it's not conspicuous'. Why did the accused take it to mean the necessity of changing the number-plates and not, for example, of taking the car to the garage, to safeguard it precisely so that no-one would be able to change those numbers?

COLONEL: It's difficult for me to take a stand on these speculations. I understood it that way, as an instruction.

OLSZEWSKI: Witness General Platek, what is your response to the accused Pietruszka's explanations, because it's important.

PLATEK: [*the first signs of uneasiness*] I did not say, I do not remember, that there was any question about the change of number. I simply gave instructions: please clarify whether this car was used or not, and all other cars with a Warsaw registration number seen in Bydgoszcz. I'd had a telephone call from my superior asking me to report on the matter urgently, so the order was issued on the run.

OLSZEWSKI: Yes, but from explanations given by the accused

Pietruszka, it clearly transpires that it concerned precisely the car number WAB 6031.

PLATEK: I don't remember, it was in a hurry, as I said, and I don't know. Later that day, after a conference of the entire investigating team—

OLSZEWSKI: Was Adam Pietruszka included in the group?

PLATEK: Yes.

OLSZEWSKI: And Piotrowski?

PLATEK: No. After the conference, one of my Colonels said he had one more issue for me and he would like to discuss it.

OLSZEWSKI: In other words, just between the two of you?

PLATEK: You could say that. He informed me that the number of the car, WAB 6031, had been verified and that it was an operational number of the Interior Ministry.

OLSZEWSKI: I take it that by an operational number you mean a false number.

PLATEK: [*ignoring the statement*] I asked Colonel Pietruszka to my room and passed on the information. I rang my superior and said: 'Comrade Minister, I must discuss something urgently with you. Can I come and see you?' At that moment, Piotrowski, I think, together with Colonel Pietruszka, walked in — I have a hazy recollection of this — and I told him that a car, which was at his disposal in the Department, had been seen on the 19th in Bydgoszcz. Piotrowski said that this must have been a misunderstanding, something of the sort. I asked Colonel Pietruszka to take him to his office so that he could write an appropriate statement on this matter.

OLSZEWSKI: Did you check up on the progress of the explanation of the car number? Did you check up on what was going on, or did you leave it to Pietruszka?

PLATEK: I've already explained this: after issuing an order in such haste I went to see my superior and returned in the evening, asked about it and then ordered other services to see to its implementation.

OLSZEWSKI: Perhaps I'd better explain the question again: did you check up on the circumstances surrounding the car with the registration number WAB 6031 — the very registration number which had been sighted in Bydgoszcz, the very registration number which you had seen in the parking lot of your own office building, the very registration number which you'd

been told was an operational number of your own Ministry —
or did you leave the checking to your deputy, namely the
accused Pietruszka?

PLATEK: I thought Colonel Pietruszka ought to check up to see
that it got done.

OLSZEWSKI: Pietruszka did not carry out your orders within
twenty-four hours. Didn't you blame him? Didn't you become
suspicious?

PLATEK: Yes, he was taking his time.

OLSZEWSKI: Did you consider him to be the most suitable person
to check that car which belonged to the Department and to
the section under his supervision?

PLATEK: To tell the truth, no-one else was free, everybody was
busy and had their instructions. But there was no reason not
to trust Pietruszka.

OLSZEWSKI: Until what moment was Pietruszka an official
member of your investigating group?

PLATEK: Up to the very — up to the moment of his detention — up
to the 2nd.

OLSZEWSKI: You saw the car on Sunday, 21st October, and you left
the investigation of it to Pietruszka up to the 2nd November?

PLATEK: Yes.

OLSZEWSKI: That was the day you yourself were suspended from
duty?

PLATEK: Yes.

OLSZEWSKI: Did you link your suspension with the fact that Pietruszka played this kind of role in the investigation?

PLATEK: I can only repeat what the Minister said to me, Your
Honour: that in connection with the investigation in progress
it would be inappropriate for me to continue my job, and he
did not make any critical comments.

OLSZEWSKI: In the written report you requested from the accused
Piotrowski, he stated that, on the day Father Popieluszko was
kidnapped, on Friday, 19th October, he had gone on a trip to
pick mushrooms. And, after receiving his report, you sent
him home. Do you believe that at the time when there were
grounds for suspicion, since you already knew it was Piotrowski's car and that therefore he'd lied in his report about
going to pick mushrooms, did you think that sending Piotrowski home was the correct decision for the good of the
investigation?

PLATEK: The fact that he wrote about mushrooms in his report was no proof that he committed the deed. Besides, I must say that we did everything to guard him.

OLSZEWSKI: Does the witness realize that it is a serious offence to let the suspect go home — that it could fundamentally affect the results of the search of Piotrowski's flat?

PLATEK: Steps securing Piotrowski had been taken.

OLSZEWSKI: Does the accused realize—?

JUDGE: [*interrupting*] I am going to order a pause. The witness is obviously tired. But I should like to take this opportunity of drawing attention to two documents which deal with actions concerned with the search for Father Popieluszko. They stress the enormous commitment shown by General Platek, and his great contribution to his organization of the search.

OLSZEWSKI: I am surprised, Your Honour, that you should draw attention to these matters during the witness's testimony. They cannot possibly constitute an integral part of it. They're just documents of no importance to this case.

[*Light on* CHROSTOWSKI.]

CHROSTOWSKI: There's another story going around. More of a rumour than a story. People say that in a room on the top floor of the hotel opposite the Court, Security people sit and monitor the proceedings. Whenever they think one of their employees needs a break, they press a button which turns on a light under the Judge's desk. The moment the Judge sees the light, he orders a pause. It's only a rumour.

[*Light on the Court.*]

MARCZUK: Did your duties on Friday, 19th October, the day Father Popieluszko was abducted, did your duties allow you to contact Piotrowski?

PLATEK: It was not possible for me to contact Piotrowski because of my work that day.

MARCZUK: The witness, Barbara Story, Piotrowski's secretary, says you tried to telephone him twice that day.

PLATEK: No, I did not.

OLSZEWSKI: If, as you have described it, the Popieluszko case was 'marginal', then why what was done to him done?

PLATEK: I have asked myself this and I haven't been able to find an answer. I cannot understand what was the aim. Piotrowski was indeed in a difficult position, under pressure from three sides: it was a national problem, perhaps colleagues outside the Department, he was also looking for legal solutions.

OLSZEWSKI: Under pressure from three sides. Could you elaborate?

PLATEK: I meant from underneath, from the top and from the side. It's just my impression.

OLSZEWSKI: On what grounds are these impressions founded?

PLATEK: I couldn't tell.

OLSZEWSKI: When did your suspicions rest on a specific individual?

PLATEK: Um . . .

JUDGE: [*being helpful*] On Monday, 22nd, in the evening, after you read Piotrowski's statement?

PLATEK: Yes. After reading the statement there was no doubt in my mind that the matter absolutely demanded an explanation.

OLSZEWSKI: Simply that — in your opinion Piotrowski was under suspicion?

PLATEK: Yes. On Tuesday the 23rd, the Minister ordered me to bring Piotrowski before him, and asked him: Did you take part in the kidnap of Father Popieluszko? Piotrowski said no, and added that he was first and foremost an employee of the Security Service and he could not have done it. The Minister ordered him to be taken to the Investigative Bureau Director.

[*Light on* CHROSTOWSKI.]

CHROSTOWSKI: So, Piotrowski, first and foremost an employee of the Security Service, is arrested. Just like that. He doesn't seem to have put up much of a fight. Why? Was it perhaps because he was so certain he would always be protected? Look, he says to himself, if it's number-plates that's worrying my superiors, I'll change them, he says, no-one'll make a fuss, no-one'll ever know. Remember, all the time the investigation's going on, the whole country's looking for Father Jerzy: police, soldiers, helicopters. Even though he knew I'd escaped from the car, that I was in police custody, that I was pointing the finger at him and his two henchmen, he still wasn't troubled. What's he thinking? He's thinking, I'll be rewarded not punished. But what he hadn't reckoned on was the shock, the grief of ordinary people all over the country, all over the world. The outrage. At some point, someone must

have said, 'We can't contain this any longer. Sacrifice Piotrowski, pull the plug on him, put him in the dock, let him
take the rap'. But who said it? The General? Someone higher
up? No-one's asked, so no-one's told. Well, whoever it was
knew what they were doing. The moment the Captain was
arrested the wall of silence crumbled. And it is now that the
body of Father Popieluszko is about to bear witness.

[*Light on the Court. The video screen begins to be put in place.*]

CHMIELEWSKI: When I heard that Piotrowski had been arrested, I
decided to tell the truth. I made a statement that we threw the
dead priest into the Vistula. I was afraid that I could be
named as the only instigator. I tried to point to places and
things which would show that I was not alone. [*stammering
uncontrollably*] Until Piotrowski's arrest, I avoided from fear,
simple fear, telling what really happened. I had to say it in the
end because one cannot live with such awareness — [*He is
almost in tears.*]

PROSECUTOR: The Prosecutor's Office has made available a video
cassette of this statement, dated 25th October.

[*On the screen: the picture flickers into life: Int. Room. Day.
Close shot of* CHMIELEWSKI. *He shows no sign of nervousness.
He speaks without a stammer and has no uncontrollable tic.*]

CHMIELEWSKI: We reached the dam at Wloclawek, where we all
threw Father Popieluszko's body into the water.

VOICE: [*off-camera*] What does 'we all' mean?

CHMIELEWSKI: It means all three of us who were present in the car.

VOICE: How did it happen?

CHMIELEWSKI: We took him out of the boot and threw him over the
railing.

VOICE: In what direction?

CHMIELEWSKI: To the left, about sixty, maybe fifty metres from the
end of the dam. I will point out the spot.

VOICE: At the moment when you threw Father Popieluszko's body
into the Vistula River, was the person alive?

CHMIELEWSKI: From what I could see, no.

VOICE: And in what circumstances did he die?

CHMIELEWSKI: As the result of losing consciousness, or after the
beatings.

VOICE: What sort of beatings?

CHMIELEWSKI: After the blows on the head.

VOICE: Who struck the blows?

CHMIELEWSKI: Piotrowski did.

VOICE: What with?

CHMIELEWSKI: With a wooden truncheon.

> [*The cassette runs out. The light begins to grow and the video screen is removed.*]

OLSZEWSKI: I would like it noted by the Court that, when this recording was made, on the 25th October, the accused Chmielewski's voice was normal and that there was no stammer.

JUDGE: I will comply with that request.

> [*The Court is again revealed. On the witness stand is* PRO-FESSOR MARIA BYRDY, *aged seventy-five, and frail in appearance. On a table near her are several grey boxes.*]

PROSECUTOR: Professor Byrdy, you performed a post-mortem on the body of Father Popieluszko?

BYRDY: Yes. I think it vital to demonstrate to the Court certain material evidence which interested us.

JUDGE: Professor, what do you propose? Where are we to start? With which objects?

> [*During the course of her evidence* BYRDY *takes the various exhibits from the boxes. She also refers to photographs.*]

BYRDY: May it please the Court, two gags are in the inventory. One was the first gag introduced into the mouth, and that is this gag here, look, with the threads separated, all disordered, you see, and fairly intensively soaked with blood and I think also with vomit, for everything is stuck together. That is the gag, a part of which protruded, there, and a part was stuffed inside the mouth.

> [*As the evidence proceeds, all the accused bow their heads, unwilling to watch the demonstration.*]

PROSECUTOR: Is the gag disordered from biting?

BYRDY: And from action by the tongue in attempts to remove it. This wad of gauze was stuffed in the mouth. And it's soaked with blood and half-digested food, which must also have been running out of Father Popieluszko's nose. This wad of gauze was sticking out of his mouth so it was covered by this sticking-plaster. It is about 51 centimetres long. It is, of course, wrinkled at the moment. If the Court will please note, it is stained, you see, all stained with blood. Here is where a wisp of hair was attached. This, then, was taped across this wad of gauze. On top of this plaster they used a roll of gauze, and then another, which encircled the priest's neck. And this was the one: it was twisted, you see. This was the one that ran round the neck.

PROSECUTOR: Could the second gag have made it effectively difficult to breathe through the nose?

BYRDY: Of course, it covered the nostrils. Consider, for example, its width. Now, here we have the constricting loop, this open loop here.

PROSECUTOR: Is that the neck loop, the noose?

BYRDY: Yes. It is an open loop. 'Open' because it only pressed half-way round the neck.

PROSECUTOR: Can you show this to us, Professor?

BYRDY: Would one of you gentlemen—?

> [*The* COURT OFFICIAL *assists her. She demonstrates on herself.*]

The legs were tied like this: it was wound round twice, or three or four times on one leg, and then the rope went to the other leg at ankle level and it was wound round again, two or three times, and then it went back in a figure of eight, so that the legs were both bound separately and with this rope in the figure of eight. There was a strong knot there, it was tied tightly and it was tied with these knots. And here, at this spot, a separate rope was tied which ran along the spine to the neck.

PROSECUTOR: Professor, the loop that was placed round the neck, was it placed so that his spine was bent backwards, or was it, well, in a straight line?

BYRDY: The way in which the loop around his neck behaved and the force of constriction depended on the movement of the limbs. If the limbs were moved, then the loop would press harder around that part of the neck.

OLSZEWSKI: Could this kind of leg-straightening movement be a reflex action in an unconscious man?

BYRDY: No. On the other hand, with any attempt to move the body by third parties, there may be situations where the rope could go a little slacker or, with the legs in another position, it could tighten up and press harder.

OLSZEWSKI: So it would depend on how the legs were arranged in the boot—?

BYRDY: That is correct—

OLSZEWSKI: [*continuing*] — when being placed there?

BYRDY: And also when being carried, moved from place to place, thrown, of course.

PROSECUTOR: Professor, you have there a wooden club. And was that perhaps the rag previously used to wrap round the object?

BYRDY: Two rags were used to wrap round the two clubs.

OLSZEWSKI: Professor, in the forensic evidence, reference was made to 'blows dealt by club or fist'. Could you tell us the sum total of blows with the club?

BYRDY: Three blows on the left arm. Further, at least two blows in the region of the corner of the mandible — [*She points to the spot on her jaw.*] It is also the club that could have caused those deep contusions of the muscles at the back of the neck, and also those rather shallow contusions in the region of the shoulders. Here we assumed at least six, so we already have at least eight blows, plus the first three, that makes eleven.

OLSZEWSKI: But in the forensic evidence there were at least thirteen.

BYRDY: Yes. There were also those in the area of the temple, at least two.

OLSZEWSKI: So, to use layman's language, those large bruises could have been caused through being hit with the club?

BYRDY: The club is sufficiently heavy, it has sufficient mass to cause the various lacerations we ascertained.

OLSZEWSKI: And what about the loss of consciousness? Could that also have been caused?

BYRDY: The loss of consciousness as well.

MARCZUK: If the club, wrapped in a rag, was used to deprive Father Popieluszko of consciousness, can one estimate the force of the blow in such a way so that only that result — unconsciousness — would be obtained, and not anything more which would have endangered his life? Is this at all possible?

BYRDY: I think, Your Honour, it was not a question of stunning alone, but of making the victim unconscious for a longer period.

[PIOTROWSKI *looks up and smiles ironically.*]

OLSZEWSKI: The manner in which Father Popieluszko was tied up was — as we have seen — very effective. Could this method of tying be done quickly? Or does it indicate that it was precise, that cold-blooded deliberation was needed and that it wasn't done in panic?

BYRDY: One could say that the second rope was used in a systematic way.

JUDGE: Let me understand this: in your first report, it was said the cause of death was strangulation by the noose. Now, am I to understand that you have revised this opinion?

BYRDY: Yes, Your Honour. Our conclusion is that all the maltreatment which the victim had to suffer caused death. In my opinion, the victim died of the beatings, the gagging *and* by strangulation with a noose. Furthermore, death was not caused by drowning, in spite of the liquid found in the lungs which was mainly vomit but which might have contributed to death by suffocation.

[*The* PROSECUTOR *nods and* BYRDY *leaves.*]

OLSZEWSKI: Accused Chmielewski. You have painted a picture of yourself as passive and reluctant to take part. You pleaded not guilty to kidnapping with particular torment. My question is: what has to be done to be able to speak of kidnapping with particular torment? Can you explain this to the Court?

CHMIELEWSKI: [*slightly inaudible and incoherent*] Perhaps this is indeed an aspect of torment.

OLSZEWSKI: And what about gagging?

CHMIELEWSKI: I did not consider gagging itself to be particular torment.

OLSZEWSKI: And what about handcuffing?

CHMIELEWSKI: This is a means of overpowering but I don't consider this to be particular torment.

OLSZEWSKI: And so, you still maintain that you are not guilty of kidnapping with particular torment?

CHMIELEWSKI: [*breaking down*] I did not gag directly, did not tie directly. I think this was horrid. [*sobbing*] It was a terrible chain of events and this is more than I can take. I believed in Piotrowski more than my own father—

[PIOTROWSKI, *moved, buries his face in his hands.*]

I knew Piotrowski. I had no grounds whatever to suppose that the whole affair might end this way. He said to me, 'Decent and appropriate people are dealing with this matter at H.Q. There is nothing to worry about'. I also have a family — people who are suffering.

MARCZUK: Defendant Pekala, you were also told that as long as the body was not recovered everything would be all right. Why then did you too decide to point to the place where the body was?

PEKALA: I understood that such a tragic end, when a man dies, cannot serve even the greatest causes. I said where the body was because I was afraid it might lead to riots.

OLSZEWSKI: But you weren't afraid of riots until after Piotrowski's arrest?

[*No response.*]

MARCZUK: Does the defendant regret his own behaviour?

PEKALA: Yes, I do regret it. I regret, simply, that I came to my senses too late and that I was, in fact, to put it this way, used. I should have had enough imagination to imagine that a man could actually die, that — [*He breaks off for a moment.*] — it unfortunately happened: what cannot be reversed, simply.

PROSECUTOR: The defendant stated during the pre-trial investigation that at a certain moment he felt cheated. Can he say why he felt cheated?

PEKALA: Firstly, that things came to this, that Piotrowski did not lead us right up to the end. Secondly, he had created a myth that this had been a decision taken on high. And thirdly, that he spoke of immunity during the action. He certainly didn't say we would go unpunished if the priest was tortured, tormented, or something like that, but he created the illusion that this would be covered up.

OLSZEWSKI: Perhaps the defendant would like to recall the oath he took on entering the service.

PEKALA: Yes.

OLSZEWSKI: Does the defendant recall today what the contents were of this oath? What did he promise at that time? What did he undertake to do?

PEKALA: To serve the homeland, defend law and order, security.

OLSZEWSKI: Did this oath also speak of observing the law?

PEKALA: Yes.

OLSZEWSKI: Thank you very much. Accused Piotrowski, what is

your attitude today to these deeds, particularly to the death of Father Popieluszko?

PIOTROWSKI: I think that, despite everything, I am still a normal person and that, in general, I react normally. We all stand here today, stripped of any kind of pride or dignity. I am certainly guilty of this death to a certain extent. I am also guilty of the suffering of the mother, whom no-one can give back her son. I dare not even ask her for any forgiveness. Waldek Chmielewski, esteemed Court, was a normal healthy man only just recently, who took joy in his kid who was beginning to walk, and also took joy in the one that is about to be born. Leszek Pekala was, only recently, a carefree man, too, and it is also difficult to shake off the nightmare that I have taken them away from their families too, that they simply lack a reason for living. I have condemned a large number of people to suffering. I cannot help thinking that my children have to take a new name to avoid the unintentional cruelty of other children. And although the law does not recognize this notion, I have condemned myself to civil death: this gives the esteemed Court an image of a kind of what I think. In any case, I would like to say that a sentence will be passed in this Court and this sentence will not affect me, for I died back on 19th October, 1984. A civil death is far worse than a physical one.

PROSECUTOR: Defendant Pietruszka, what is your attitude now?

COLONEL: I may be blamed for many things, carelessness in dressing, carelessness in management, but to accept an action which ends with Father Popieluszko getting into the car — that is inadmissible from the methodological point of view. It does not fall into the cardinal methods of work organization. Apparently, I agree to this type of action, and that Waldemar Chmielewski should take part in it, an employee whose father is more than a friend to me — that I should send his son, whom I brought into this work myself — that I should send him on this mission. I understand that one could reverse the reasoning, but my connections with Chmielewski Senior made such a thing unacceptable.

PIOTROWSKI: [an outburst] Esteemed Court, I would like to express my views on the explanations generally given by my former boss. If I was asked to assess his positive traits, I would mention one special trait, namely his cunning. I would say that this is his number one trait if it were not for the fact that he hasn't succeeded in covering up all the traces of this whole business. I am, however, aware of the fact that once this whole tragedy happened I did not retract one little bit in order to shed responsibility. This is no masochism, no playing the boy-scout. This is simply my idea of honour. I would like to stress that Colonel Pietruszka's explanations on issues of fundamental importance are a lie.

OLSZEWSKI: Throughout the pre-trial investigation all four accused referred to their superiors as 'the top'. But now, in Court, their testimony seems to have changed. Accused Chmielewski, you said that Piotrowski had told you the action had been agreed with Deputy-Minister Ciaston who is, I believe, also head of the Security Service. Is that, perhaps, what was meant by 'the top'?

CHMIELEWSKI: Piotrowski merely said that the Colonel had to agree the matter with those above. The name Ciaston I added for myself mentally.

PIOTROWSKI: The Colonel said to me, regarding the action against the priest, 'Comrade, this is a decision from the highest level'. I was convinced it couldn't just be the Colonel's idea. I believed the decision would, at least, have to be taken at departmental level. I said this to my subordinates. It may be in this connection I said that this only could be a deputy-minister. But I understand now that it was only the Colonel's approval and to mention other names would be to incriminate innocent persons.

OLSZEWSKI: Defendant Pietruszka, what did you mean, 'a decision at the highest level'? You implied that there was, before the kidnapping, evidence that your superiors, that 'the top' were interested in this case. Whom did you mean by 'the top'?

COLONEL: The material proof of the interest of our superiors in cases where the activities of certain clergy were monitored was that in the more drastic cases, protests forwarded to the Episcopate or to particular bishops were signed by the Deputy Minister. On the basis of such facts I formulated the opinion that our superiors were interested in this case. I did not use the expression 'the top' as meaning my superiors because in the Department I also — perhaps somewhat immodestly — believed myself to be the top.

PROSECUTOR: Accused Piotrowski, please answer this question

now: without the inspiration of the defendant Pietruszka, would the accused have undertaken the action on 19th October?

PIOTROWSKI: Definitely not.

COLONEL: Esteemed Court, you must understand that Piotrowski had certain traits which could be called insubordination. He often reported on what he had already done. And he himself has greatly emphasized his personal commitment to his work. He was not interested in the administrative side of the job. He found it boring. He is a relatively young man and this could change with time. That is why he was promoted and enjoyed a good reputation. Because one should believe in man. In the Marxist view, man is the greatest good. One should have faith in man. What else have we got left?

[*Light on* CHROSTOWSKI.]

CHROSTOWSKI: Other things emerge about these men. Chmielewski. He says he became ill two days after the murder. Not so. He's perfectly all right a whole week later, as the Court noted. Because what causes his collapse is not remorse or guilt, but the shock of finding himself in Court. It's coming into the light that shocks the system. And the boy-scout, Piotrowski. It turns out he's something of a car-dealer. He imports an Audi from West Germany but puts it in his father-in-law's name. He also gets a Fiat 132 from abroad but doesn't pay customs duty on it. And in return for getting the Audi serviced free of charge, he wangles a passport for the mechanic who wants to travel to West Germany. Cars play a big part in his life. In 1983, he runs over and kills a woman crossing a road. He doesn't report the accident. So, what happens? Charges against him are dropped and his superiors have 'a disciplinary conversation' with him. That's for accidentally killing a woman. All this comes out in Court. And talking of fathers. And mothers. Piotrowski is the son of a police colonel, who was one of the highest-ranking police officers in Stalinist times. His mother was the Governor of the Fordon prison for women. Some say it's the toughest in the country. Both parents are retired. But now, it's up to the lawyers.

[*Light on the Court.*]

PROSECUTOR: May it please the Court, this trial is drawing to a close. It is a trial that will go down in the history of the social-ist administration of justice in this country as not just one of a murder full of shocking descriptions, but a trial for the complete fulfilment of the shape of socialist administration of justice in this country, for universal respect of the law and the good name of the Polish People's Republic. Citizen Judges! People would be wrong to assume that because the accused were officials of the Interior Ministry they committed these crimes. Just the opposite is true: they committed these crimes because they departed from the norms and principles of behaviour which the officials of this Ministry are obliged to observe. Cynicism characterizes all the defendants. They make a mockery of all moral standards. Regarding the accused, Piotrowski, this cold and cruel man, in the face of his repulsive moral attitude, the severest of words come to one's lips. In a law-abiding state, such as ours, nothing can justify lynch law which leads to anarchy and weakens the state. Objectively speaking, lynch law deals a painful blow at the political line. Father Jerzy Popieluszko acted against this line. As a chaplain he spoke of struggle against the system, the state and its bodies. He sowed hatred and showered abuse. As a citizen and a priest he took extreme actions which ran counter to the principles of the law. He fell victim to the defendants who, in the same way as him, considered that they had a mission to undertake activities outside the law. Like Father Popieluszko, they thought that the offices they held would protect them. However, although Father Popieluszko had reason to think his superiors would show tolerance, the defendants could not and ought not to have expected this. Let me now say something about such vague expressions as the 'top' or the 'top echelons' which do not make it possible to apply them to anyone in particular. This trial has shown that the 'top' or 'top echelon' are not to be found in the Ministry of Internal Affairs. It follows, therefore, that persons or centres inside the country who are actively opposed to the political line of the Ninth Congress of the Polish Communist Party — a line consistently implemented by the government of General Jaruzelski — might have desired this sort of provoca-tion and might have exploited its consequences for their own political ends. There are also foreign centres who for a long time now have been acting against the interest of the state, a number of them inspired and paid for by the special services of certain capitalist states. May it please the Court, Citizen Judges: punishment is a straightforward function whereby guilt is recognized. Although the accused did not act because of base reasons nevertheless their actions were premeditated, ruthless and cruel. I, therefore, demand for the defendants Pekala, Chmielewski and Pietruszka, twenty-five years' imprisonment. For the defendant Piotrowski, I demand the penalty of death.

OLSZEWSKI: May it please the Provincial Court, my situation is particularly difficult because what is said in this court-room constantly calls up the shade of the victim, a person who mattered to me, whom I knew, whom I valued and with whom certain matters sometimes linked me. It is difficult for me, finally, because the demand by the Prosecutor for the supreme penalty hangs over this court-room. I, as an Auxiliary Prosecutor, can permit myself the luxury of not speaking on this subject, of not saying whether I personally am for or against it, but I cannot forget the person who was murdered: that person, I know for sure, would have been against it. Even though public opinion cries out for the supreme punishment in this case, let the Court note that, all his life, the victim opposed the death penalty. But now, I must strongly protest against the attacks on Father Popieluszko. The fact that a Prosecutor equated the victim with his murderers went beyond what was permissible and was unique in legal chronicles throughout the world. May it please the Court, the defendants thought they were above the law and now plead political motives. It seems to me that the real motives of all the accused were linked to the desire for an official career. They had a peculiar understanding of such a career. The Prosecutor has said that this matter was a political provocation. I share this assessment. But who is interested in this country being a country of misery, despair and terror? The weakness of some always becomes the strength of others. Who profited when Poland was weak? Any child can answer that question provided he's conscientiously taught the history of his native land. I shudder to think that the defendants could act with full awareness of the damage their action might do to the motherland. The defendants have said they felt cheated because the guarantees of impunity turned out to be illusory. I wish they understood they have been deceived a hundred times more because, with their own hands, in foreign interests, they could by their actions poison with hatred their native country. But the aim of the crime has not been achieved. Not evil, but good has prevailed. History will show whether the four defendants were the only ones responsible. One has to hope that those in power will never be so weak as to avail themselves of crime in order to carry out their aims.

PROSECUTOR: Your Honour, the lawyer, Olszewski, protested against my equating the victim with the murderers. This is totally unjustified slander. The Prosecutor's Office has treated the murderers with all severity — both for the deed and the motives. It is impermissible, however, to obscure the substratum of this crime. It is political in nature. The statement that certain extreme political attitudes brought about certain other extreme political attitudes — is this not a truth without which it is impossible to understand anything of the crimes being judged here? There is a suggestion that everything done by a priest is good and noble, that all priests have always served the nation well. It has not always been so. The crime cannot be properly judged without an appraisal of the activities of the priest. We, Your Honour, raise the motives and circumstances of the accused in this Court not in order to justify their crime, but because it is our duty at least to try to understand those motives and circumstances.

[*He sits.* CHROSTOWSKI *turns to the audience.*]

CHROSTOWSKI: And last, it's the turn of the Judge.

JUDGE: I pronounce sentence. Could all those present in the courtroom please rise? In the name of the Polish People's Republic, the Torun Provincial Court has considered the case of: Grzegorz Piotrowski, born on 23rd May, 1951; background: from the intelligentsia, married with two children, with a higher education, a mathematician; of Leszek Pekala, born on 30th May, 1952; background: from the intelligentsia, a bachelor, with a higher education, an electronics specialist; of Waldemar Marek Chmielewski, born 28th February, 1955; background: from the intelligentsia, married, with one child, with a higher education, a political scientist; of Adam Pietruszka, born on 19th July, 1938, coming from a peasant family, married with one grown-up child, with a higher education, lawyer. The Provincial Court pronounces all the defendants guilty as charged. I sentence: the defendant Grzegorz Piotrowski to 25 years' imprisonment and deprivation of civil rights for a period of 10 years; the defendant Leszek Pekala to 15 years' imprisonment; the defendant Waldemar Marek Chmielewski to 14 years' imprisonment; the defendant Adam Pietruszka to 25 years' imprisonment and deprivation of civil rights for a period of 10 years. I hereby close the proceedings of the Torun Provincial Court.

[*Light on* CHROSTOWSKI.]

CHROSTOWSKI: Random facts which may be of interest. It's now known that Miroslaw Milewski, the Central Committee Secretary responsible for security questions, stopped attending meetings of the Politburo and the Central Committee. He was taking what is called 'a long, recuperative vacation'. He has now resigned. There's also a rumour that General Platek has been put in charge of Customs and Excise. And here's another story. Question: Why did Piotrowski get 25 years? Answer: One year for murdering Father Popieluszko, 24 for screwing it up.

[*Behind him, now, light grows on the boot section of a Fiat. Inside it is a crib.*]

As far as I'm concerned, the motive for this crime was to remove Father Popieluszko from our lives. But, in a sense, they achieved the opposite. Every evening, at seven o'clock, a Mass is said for him in his church. And outside the church, in the boot of a Fiat motor-car, there's a crib. People put flowers there. It's an act of remembrance.

[*He places a single flower on the witness box.*]

[*He exits.*]

POPIELUSZKO'S VOICE: We can overcome fear only if we accept suffering in the name of a greater value. Christ told his followers: 'Be not afraid of them that kill the body, and after that have no more that they can do'

[*Lights fade.*]

THE END

Other books by Ronald Harwood

Novels:
All the Same Shadows
The Guilt Merchants
The Girl in Melanie Klein
Articles of Faith
The Genoa Ferry
Cesar and Augusta

Short Stories:
One. Interior. Day. *Adventures in the Film Trade*

Biography:
Sir Donald Wolfit CBE: *His life and work in the unfashionable theatre**

Plays:
A Family
The Ordeal of Gilbert Pinfold (from Evelyn Waugh)*
The Dresser*
After the Lions*
Tramway Road*

Screenplays:
One Day in the Life of Ivan Denisovich (with introduction)

Miscellaneous:
A Night at the Theatre (Editor)
The Ages of Gielgud (Editor)
All the World's a Stage

* *Published by Amber Lane Press*